TWELVE

AND A HALF

Also by Gary Vaynerchuk

*Crushing It! How Great Entrepreneurs Build Their
Business and Influence—And How You Can, Too*

*Jab, Jab, Jab, Right Hook: How to Tell Your
Story in a Noisy Social World*

*#AskGaryVee: One Entrepreneur's Take on
Leadership, Social Media, and Self-Awareness*

The Thank You Economy

Crush It!: Why NOW Is the Time to Cash In on Your Passion

TWELVE
AND A HALF

Leveraging the Emotional
Ingredients Necessary for
Business Success

Gary Vaynerchuk

HARPER
BUSINESS

An Imprint of HarperCollins*Publishers*

HarperCollins books may be purchased for educational, business, or sales promotional use. For information, please email the Special Markets Department at SPsales@harpercollins.com.

FIRST EDITION

Library of Congress Cataloging-in-Publication Data has been applied for.

ISBN 978-0-06-267468-5
ISBN 978-0-06-314379-1 (International Edition)

21 22 23 24 25 LSC 10 9 8 7 6 5 4 3 2 1

Dedicated to every single entrepreneur, founder, executive, manager, employee, mom, dad, and older sibling courageous enough to become better leaders to those who look up to them.

CONTENTS

INTRODUCTION

Years ago, I had the most difficult conversation with a client that I've ever had to have in the course of my career.

It was with a top executive from one of the biggest brands we were working with at VaynerMedia, a contemporary creative and media agency where I'm the CEO. The executive called me and asked if we could meet in Midtown Manhattan. She wanted to talk face-to-face.

That day, an entry-level employee at my company had accidentally posted a tweet from the client's Twitter account, thinking she was logged into her personal account. It was a very negative tweet about another agency that VaynerMedia was working with to support the brand. To the world, it looked as if the brand had made disparaging comments about the other agency.

It was a very quick meeting. The executive told me that she expected this not to happen again and asked me to put the proper protocols and systems in place to ensure that.

Then she said to me, "The only way our company sees that we can go forward working together is if you fire the individual who posted that tweet."

It took me about a hundredth of a second to think it through.

I said to her, "I can't do that."

I had to be able to run my own business and make my own decisions about my employees. The executive had every ability to fire us if that's what she felt was necessary. But it had to be my decision what the ramifications of that tweet would be.

She was surprised. That brand represented about 30 percent of our total revenue at the time.

I was mentally prepared for them to fire us, but at the time, I knew that we had just enough new business coming in that we could afford a year with no profit. I also had enough saved up that, if we lost money that year, I was willing to help bridge the gap if needed. If we could weather that storm, it would be a clear indicator to our employees as to what we really value.

This conversation was one of those interesting moments when you have to decide what you're going to stand for. We scheduled a call the next day, and I stood my ground. Luckily, the client didn't fire us.

I tell that story because modern society's definition of a "smart business decision" is disproportionately predicated on analytics. Business leaders tend to find safety in the "black-and-white." They find safety in the academics, math, hard data, and what looks good on spreadsheets.

It's harder to gauge the 30-, 60-, 90-, 365-, or even 730-day effectiveness of empathy, kindness, and self-awareness in an organization, but their results will play out. When you can eliminate fear from your organization, very good things happen. If employees don't have to spend their time trying to outmaneuver one another, trying to kill one another politically, they may actually achieve the task at hand. I don't know which six-year-old girl in Tennessee is going to invent the system to score this, but at some point, it will be mappable. This level of common sense and human truth will play out.

In big companies especially, many decisions are predicated on ninety-day numbers. That practice comes from Wall Street and business school, where you're being judged every quarter on performance. It can lead to short-term behavior, even though many of us are still planning to be in business over the next five, ten, twenty, or even fifty-plus years.

Unfortunately, the bias toward short-term metrics can also make emotional intelligence a "nice to have" rather than a requirement. It creates a scenario in which a leader looks the other way when one employee makes everyone else in the office miserable, just because that employee happens to be bringing in the most revenue. It makes people think negative behavior and a poor EQ (emotional quotient) are just side effects of being "good at business."

The business world I entered in the late nineties put the black-and-white on a pedestal. At that time, it wasn't recognized that soft skills could be the key to building a successful company. I don't recall hearing these traits being emphasized in the mainstream business community. Business was "dog-eat-dog," an endeavor where "only the strong survive."

Ironically, I *also* believe that only the strong survive. I just believe that leaning into your humanity is the actual strength that will help you survive and flourish. *Not* yelling at someone else in a conference room. *Not* being a tough negotiator with aggressive words. To this day, I think the strongest person is someone who's able to deploy kindness in the face of the opposite. The twelve ingredients I describe in this book (we'll get to what the half means later) are some of the traits that have led to my success and happiness over the years, in addition to others that I've observed and admired: gratitude, self-awareness, accountability, optimism, empathy, kindness, tenacity, curiosity, patience, conviction, humility, and ambition. The black-and-white is still wildly important, but in my opinion, it's a distant second to mastering soft skills.

I couldn't be more aware that there are fifteen to fifty other ingredients that could've made it into this book. But these twelve stood out to me after seeing other leaders fall short in deploying them and how that gap made people around them feel. Many people in conference halls, dinners, lunches, buses, and flights would tell me stories of these twelve ingredients being neglected. One of the sad things about human nature is that negativity is louder than positivity. It's been one of the driving forces of my life to make positivity louder. One of the reasons I'm writing this book is to cheer for these traits and put a spotlight on them in business.

My greatest challenge has been extracting these ingredients and articulating them. They're not tangible. They can't be tracked or measured on a spreadsheet. In fact, in May 1998, when I walked into my dad's liquor store, I didn't understand their significance.

My dad's not a big talker, but on Thanksgiving weekend in 2020, when I had started writing this book, he told me that he hadn't believed in "company culture" back when I first started working with him. Coming from the Soviet Union, he thought that fear and money were the most effective motivators. That's how he drove his career. But today? Now he believes in positive company culture over everything. Even though it doesn't come naturally to him and he struggles in explaining it to his friends, he told me that he knows it's crucial. I find it poetic, especially if you realize how rarely my dad tells me stuff like that.

This book is cathartic for me because it allows me to do what I can't on social media, given the fragmentation of my communication style. I think humility is one of the biggest reasons for my success, yet if you watch a one-minute video of me pontificating with uncanny conviction around an opportunity within a TikTok environment, you might say, "Fuck this know-it-all." As you'll find, you can be humble and curious but also have conviction in your beliefs. It's not either-or.

In part II, you'll see me combine these twelve ingredients into complete "meals" and show you how they can be used together when you face different challenges in business. For example, accountability and conviction are often seen as opposites to empathy and kindness; they're traits that have more "teeth." Traits like humility and conviction, ambition and patience, and gratitude and accountability might also be interpreted as opposites. This book will help you understand how many ingredients that might *seem* like opposites actually work together.

Developing these twelve ingredients individually is the starting point, but knowing how to cook the meal is the real takeaway. Even if you have all twelve in a solid place naturally or you were lucky enough to have learned some of them by experience, you still have to know how to use them together. You still need to be the "chef" who "cooks" them.

There's a time and a place for a Big Mac, but I wouldn't serve a Big Mac if I were planning a meal for twenty-five strict vegans. Every dish you make needs to be made in the context of the situation it's being served in. These twelve traits have to be used in different mixtures in every business scenario. That's all I'm ever doing.

Let's say you're the head of a law firm and you've hired a kid who grew up on "the other side of the tracks." He or she doesn't know the protocols for a fancy dinner with a client, and you end up losing the deal as a result. This is where you have to pull gratitude and accountability from the "spice rack." You need to be thankful for even having the opportunity to own a business and land this new account. You show accountability by realizing that you're the one who hired but failed to properly train that person. All of a sudden, everything else becomes secondary.

It's impossible for any of these twelve ingredients to work without patience at the core. If you're baking a pie, patience is the crust. People might think ambition contradicts patience, but I think patience is the path to your ambitions.

People often don't achieve their ambitions because of their own insecurity. In their desperation to put wins on the board so the audience claps for them, they end up taking shortcuts. It's hard for such people to build a meaningful business because they're so focused on making a million dollars and buying clothes, boats, and other fancy things without having cultivated patience.

Whatever you do professionally is normally going to be something that will take up most of your life, so patience is a practical way to get to your ambition. Lack of patience is a huge vulnerability, and it has led to more bad decisions than any other factor.

Sometimes, I notice this with my buyers at Wine Library when we make decisions and negotiate deals. It's imperative to realize that the sellers we're buying wine from are going to be our partners for the next fifty years. That's why I've left dollars on the table when negotiating a wine deal. If I had ground the sellers to the bone every time, they wouldn't have had the same relationship with me, and there would have been fewer opportunities in the future.

This was something I observed early in my career with one of our buying managers, who was a formidable negotiator. As I watched our relationships with the wine suppliers, I noticed that (1) they reacted to the buying manager's negotiation style by raising the starting price, and (2) they started taking their wines to other stores. By leaving some dollars on the table, I got many more of the best wines and had a better starting point in every negotiation.

As a CEO or manager, you also need patience as you watch your employees develop. Many of my partners and hires didn't start out great in the role they became best at.

Most important, you need to be patient with yourself as you develop these ingredients. Those who think they're running out of time get frantic and become vulnerable to bad decisions. When I was watching *The Queen's Gambit* on Netflix, I noticed that as the chess timer got lower and lower, players got more frantic. When I watched videos of the greatest chess players, I noticed the same thing. Their body language and decision making became more frantic when time became part of the equation.

I believe the majority of people starting and building businesses do not have a good relationship with time. They misunderstand it. They're basing their choices on low-probability events, like getting hit by a bus. They forget that they may live to ninety or a hundred as life expectancy increases. Patience has kept me from dwelling on bad deals I've made and allowed me to work in a family business when I wasn't making the salary I could've been making elsewhere. It's what has allowed me to take steps backward in the micro and macro without getting crippled by discouragement.

I think I have a lot more time to play. Whether that's actually true or not, I feel an enormous amount of day-to-day happiness as a result of that belief.

MY HALF: KIND CANDOR

Patience and ambition, gratitude and accountability, empathy and conviction—I balance a lot of these traits in mixtures. I've started to work on balancing my kindness with candor. I realized that kindness *without* candor was creating entitlement within my organization. By giving positive reinforcement again and again without critical feedback, I created delusion, which led to entitlement.

I have a visceral reaction to confrontation, and so I was very bad at giving critical feedback for most of my career. After twenty-four years as a business operator, I'm heartbroken that there are people out there who don't feel great toward me because I wasn't able to be candid with them. I would fire them without giving them enough feedback, or I would create situations that forced them to quit.

I didn't see the beauty of candor, the humanity in it. I didn't realize that candor actually is kindness. I can think of many times when some kind candor would've taken my success to a higher plane. All my unhappiness in life and business has resulted from my inability to deploy kind candor when necessary. That's why I'm calling it my half. I say "half" because nobody's a zero on anything. No matter how bad you think you are, the fact that you're even aware of a weakness or a gap has already started your process of becoming better at the underdeveloped skill.

My half convinces me of the importance of the other twelve ingredients. Knowing that I'm not good at kind candor yet, at least at the level of being able to cook the whole meal, makes me realize that lack of any one of the twelve is going to hurt you. It's going to limit you. It's the indicator of your vulnerabilities.

As you go through this book, I don't want you to be depressed when you find out what your halves are. I want you to be thrilled because, as you improve on those halves, more good things will happen for you. You might realize that you're unhappy because you don't have kindness to give. You might start understanding why you yell at your interns. You might start uncovering reasons why you're being selfish at work. You might learn that you're not "full." Personally, I feel grateful to be working on kind candor, a tremendous addition to the other twelve ingredients.

The growth potential of most businesses is limited by the emotional intelligence of their leaders. That goes for sports teams, families, and sovereign nations. Every single person who has a child is a leader. Anyone who has a younger sibling is a leader. Anyone who has a pet is a leader. Anybody who has even one person to manage is a leader.

This book will help you refine your ingredients and improve your leadership capabilities. The quality of your dish depends on the quality of your ingredients and the way you use them in combination.

All twelve are important. If one ingredient is secondary to another, the dish won't be good. What's more important, the fish or the salt? What's more important in baking a cake, the flour or the eggs? The answer is always both. They're equally valuable but must be deployed in different proportions in different situations. As you navigate every second of your life, you need to add different ingredients at different times.

So much has worked for me in creating outsized success because I got twelve of these down. The reason I didn't have every dish tasting perfect was that kind candor was missing.

How This Book Is Structured

As you begin part I, you'll notice that I define each ingredient and explain how it can affect your career and your life as a whole. I'm emphasizing a key concept, which may be the most important sentence in this book: *When you actually understand how unimportant business is in the grand scheme of your life, it allows you to enjoy it and potentially get better at it.* People think of me as an entrepreneur and businessman, but if I were melted down and read in book form, I think most people would be shocked to see how little I ultimately care about business.

Before you get into the following pages, you need to know that when you value life as a whole over success in business, the game gets dramatically easier and wildly more enjoyable. When you put happiness over money, stock shares, and public admiration, your day-to-day work becomes sustainable over the long haul. I believe some entrepreneurs, managers, and founders of successful businesses sometimes go through burnouts and crashes because they haven't implemented these ingredients.

In part II, I'll take you through a variety of different real-life scenarios to show how these ingredients can be used together in varying mixtures. You'll also have the chance to reflect on your reactions to challenging situations in your career and what you would do differently today with what you've learned from this book.

In part III, I'll give you real-life exercises to help you develop each ingredient, including kind candor. These exercises will enhance your conviction around your strengths and help you identify insecurities, uncover your halves, and grow in those areas. For a full list of supplemental resources, visit garyvee.com/twelveandahalfbook.

It's a shockingly simple point of view. I think of business as an art. I think it can be as beautiful as a symphony or a painting when executed properly.

For it to ever have that place in society, we must realize how the twelve and a half emotional ingredients in this book can be the catalysts for success in business.

PART I

The Emotional Ingredients

GRATITUDE

The quality of being thankful; readiness to show
appreciation for and to return kindness.[1]

I f there were a list that ranked everyone on Earth in terms of
overall success and happiness (from 1 to 7.7 billion), where do
you think you'd rank?

Write down your answer here: _____ out of 7.7 billion.

Got your number? Great.

According to the World Health Organization, 785 million people globally lack basic drinking-water services.[2] That's a little over

10 percent of the world's population, and even two million Americans don't have access to safe drinking water or basic plumbing.[3]

Do you have enough food to eat every day?

More than 820 million people in the world were undernourished in 2018.[4]

No matter how much you hate your job, do you have even the slightest potential or ability to get another one? According to the Global Slavery Index, 40.3 million people were in modern-day slavery in 2016.[5] They *really* don't have the option to quit.

Do you have a proper toilet at home? Around 60 percent of the world's people (4.5 billion of them) don't have a toilet that properly manages human waste.[6]

Do you have high-speed Internet at home? About three billion people aren't even *on* the Internet.[7] Even twenty-one million Americans lack broadband access.[8]

And we haven't even started talking about income yet. According to CNN's Davos 2017 Global Wage Calculator, the global adjusted average annual wage is $20,328.[9] In Russia, it's about $5,457 per year; in Brazil, $4,659; in India, $1,666; and in Malawi, $1,149.

Obviously, there are too many variables to identify your exact rank out of 7.7 billion. However, by throwing all this data at you, I hope to get you to understand what's actually going on in the world outside your direct surroundings.

I'm completely driven by perspective and gratitude. I was born in the former Soviet Union in Belarus, so I deeply understand how much worse life could be. In fact, I might not have even been able to get out, had it not been for the following event:

In 1970, sixteen Russians plotted to hijack a small plane. The crew pretended they were going to a wedding but secretly planned to fly the plane to Sweden to escape the Soviet Union. Their eventual goal was to arrive in Israel. But the plan didn't work out, and the participants got arrested and thrown in jail for treason.

However, that event drew global attention to the human-rights issues in the Soviet Union during the Cold War. The media in the United States covered the hijacking plot, and it changed the political landscape. Due to the increased attention and pressure, the Soviet Union loosened its regulations and eventually let more Jews leave.

I believe those sixteen people changed the course of my life.

Luck is an interesting word. I probably would attribute most of my success to my tenacity, ambition, and other emotional ingredients rather than luck, but the fact that I was able to escape the Soviet Union at a young age certainly involved luck.

People don't understand the reality of what's happening in the world because their communities are so insular. Many people look at a million dollars as the *entry point* of success. Many twenty-somethings are trying to "make it" before thirty. When you're living in a Los Angeles apartment or a house in Greenwich, Connecticut, it's tough to wrap your head around the fact that women in Africa collectively spend two hundred million hours a day collecting water.[10] People look upward at those who rank higher, but they don't look downward at the billions ranked lower.

Anybody who owns a business in a First World nation is already living an extraordinary life. I don't think most entrepreneurs realize how blessed they are. Even if it's a grind. Even if it's hard. Even if there are bad days.

Don't forget—over half the world doesn't even have a real toilet.

When you develop perspective, the timelines you set for your goals naturally shift. As I write this, life expectancy in the United

States is about seventy-nine years. In 1930, it was fifty-eight. In 1880, it was thirty-nine.[11]

Although 1880 feels like a long time ago, it really isn't. A grandparent who's ninety-one in 2021 probably knew of family members who died at thirty-nine or so. If you lived during that time, of course you needed to have your life figured out by thirty. You'd die nine years later!

Even in 1930, people died at fifty-eight. By age thirty, their lives were already more than half over.

As our life expectancies increase, shouldn't our timelines for goals increase too? Shouldn't you be OK with not having everything figured out until later?

With advances in modern medicine, I believe many of you will live to ninety or a hundred years old. If you're twenty-seven and hate your job after working your way up for five years, it's fine to take a step backward and find another job. If you're thirty-three and decide to start your own business from scratch after getting a degree in something you're not passionate about, you're not "too late." You're actually the luckiest of the lucky. You get to be alive during an era when the math shows you probably have another sixty years to play. Regardless of what happened yesterday or every day before that, you still have a generous amount of time ahead of you.

Be thoughtful and honest with yourself about your missteps, but don't start dwelling on them. People beat themselves up and obsess about something that happened thirteen years ago—a business partnership that didn't work out, a startup that failed, or a boss they didn't like—and it becomes the jail they live in. With all the time you have left, there's zero value in getting bogged down there. If I ever get into that mud, I'm grabbing my gratitude hose to wash it off.

I've had major disappointments in my career that I've dwelled on for maybe an hour. Maybe a day, if it was really a gut punch. How can I be upset about such a small thing for so long? I'm playing my life's mission. I'm doing my thing. Of course I'm going to lose every now and then. It's like losing a playoff series in basketball. It's going to happen. In the face of disappointment, gratitude is my chess move to limit dwelling on it.

Actually, as long as we're talking about dwelling, I need some help: send an e-mail to gratitude@veefriends.com, and title it "The value of dwelling." I need to know what it is.

I'm not talking about the value of mourning. I'm not saying you shouldn't give yourself time to mourn. I just think we should reserve mourning for the death of people, not bad business decisions. What's the value of dwelling? What could possibly be productive about beating yourself up for weeks, months, or years over a bad outcome?

I get it. Susan broke your heart in college, but it's over. She's forty-seven now, with three children.

One of the biggest points I'm trying to make in this book is that positive emotional ingredients provide more sustainable fuel than negative ones. If you draw energy from gratitude, you'll find that it lasts much longer than energy drawn from insecurity, anger, or disappointment.

I understand why people like to use the dark side as energy. I love being an underdog and having a chip on my shoulder too. Why do you think I love being a fan of the New York Knicks and the New York Jets? I love losing. I'm motivated by it. But I'm more motivated by the light than the dark. That balance matters.

Anger can give you a short-term energy boost, whether it's anger toward yourself or others, but once you achieve the gratification you're looking for, you'll often find that it's not as fruitful as you imagined it to be. A lot of people are motivated to "stick it" to their parents for doubting them, but by the time they do it, things are different. The situation has often changed, the parents are no longer around, or maybe they've mellowed. Insecurity and anger can be tremendous drivers of success—but I don't believe they lead to happiness.

Anger and resentment are heavy ingredients to carry around. Gratitude is light.

I'm fascinated that people think that gratitude creates complacency. There's a reason why *complacent* and *grateful* are two different words. The definition of *complacency* is "a feeling of smug or uncritical satisfaction with oneself or one's achievements."[12] They're not the same.

For example, I can separate my gratitude from my requirements for the financial structure of a business deal. If those requirements aren't getting fulfilled, I know I'm in control of making a decision on whether I sign the deal or not. Same thing applies if you work at a company: you can be grateful that you have a job, but if you feel it isn't paying you enough after you've delivered results for three years, you can take another job instead of dwelling on it.

As you'll see in part II, you can be grateful *and* ambitious. You can be grateful *and* tenacious. These traits don't have to come at the expense of one another.

Want to know where my energy and smiles come from when you see me on social media? They come from gratitude. If I wake up in the morning and nobody I love has passed away or come down with a terminal illness, then my day starts off great. If the people closest to me are OK, I'm good. I won. Nothing else can truly faze me beyond that.

If you're truly grateful for what you have instead of being envious of what you don't have, you'll be a dominant force in business and, way more important, in life.

SELF-AWARENESS

Conscious knowledge of one's own character,
feelings, motives, and desires.[13]

I f there's anything that I could wish upon society aside from
good health, it would be a new drug to help everyone develop
these emotional ingredients. If I were the FDA, the first one I would
prioritize would be self-awareness.

The value of self-awareness first hit my radar in 2011 to 2013
during the explosion of interest in entrepreneurship in popular culture. When I saw some students and executives become startup
founders, it struck me—how do they not realize that they have no

chance? Why are they trying to be a number-one (a CEO)? How do they not realize that they're better suited to be a number-two, number-three, or a number-twenty-seven player in an organization? Do they not realize that they're making this jump because they think it's cool, instead of doing it because it's their calling?

There are many reasons why humans try to become someone they're not. Sometimes, it's just delusion. (I don't say that in anger; I say it with empathy.) Delusional people lack awareness about their strengths and weaknesses.

However, what surprised me was that many of them aren't delusional—they're actually very self-aware. They do recognize they have no shot, so they overcompensate for their insecurities by propping themselves up with a job title like CEO. They'd rather put "entrepreneur" in their Instagram bios to appear successful in the eyes of the world than lean into their strengths and passions and start building sustainable, long-term happiness.

Many of those who dream of being entrepreneurs today would've dreamed of being astronauts and pilots back in 1957 or rock stars in 1975.

Self-awareness has a close relationship with self-love and self-acceptance. I'm realizing right now that it's one thing to be self-aware. It's another thing to look in the mirror and say, "Hey, you're not good at X." That doesn't mean telling yourself you're a piece of shit. It just means acknowledging a weakness.

Insecurity often leads to avoidance. People tend to be the most avoidant with their own flaws.

If you tell yourself, "You're not good at running a business," that doesn't mean you'll never have a successful, fulfilling career. Maybe you can build a personal brand for yourself as an influencer. Maybe you can make your impact as an executive. Maybe the reason you're not good at running a business is that you don't enjoy managing people, and you can bring in a partner with a complementary skill set.

When you fully accept yourself, you're no longer scared of other people. On social media and in real life, humans tend to feel uncomfortable when they feel out of place. They feel that others are superior or that an insecurity they're trying to hide will be exposed. For me, a combination of self-awareness and humility is why I love being around people. Nobody scares me.

Therefore, I don't feel the need to use my ambition as a crutch to get acceptance from others. Self-acceptance helps one embrace self-awareness, not avoid it.

For a lot of people, a little more self-awareness could help them be more secure in their titles at work. Outside of the financial benefits that can come with more senior roles, chasing titles is one hundred percent tied to caring what others in the organization think of you. For me, the job title has been an afterthought in many of the companies I'm involved with. What I care about is bringing value to every single person I interact with.

I will say, out of fairness, that your job title does become an important leverage point when you plan a move to a different company. When people in my company meet with me and ask for a different title that I can't provide, I often tell them to come back to me when they want a different job, and I'll give them a double title increase to leverage on LinkedIn.

But within the organization? Those who care too much about job titles are largely worried about other people's opinions.

Looking back, I see I've always had self-awareness, even in my youth. I knew I was a businessman, a purebred entrepreneur. When

I made a thousand dollars as a sixth grader selling stuff, I knew I was going to be OK even if I got D's and F's in school. It wasn't just my opinion that I was a talented businessman—I had affirmation from the market.

I was an entrepreneur then, and I'll still be an entrepreneur if and when it stops being cool a decade from now.

Confidence makes self-awareness easier. I'm willing to take a hard look in the mirror and acknowledge all the problems I have in my life. I'm willing to separate who I am from who I wish I could be, a challenge for those who are insecure.

The best part of acknowledging your weaknesses is that you can then start navigating around them. For example, I don't have the work ethic to put up a painting on a wall, because I don't like doing it. So, I'll find someone else to do it.

But I do have the work ethic to spend fifteen hours a day on my business, because I love it.

I can't read long texts or e-mails, so I have quick five-to-fifteen-minute meetings with my team instead. I don't say to myself, "Oh no, I need to get a tutor." Instead of taking my reading skills from bad to OK, I'd rather spend that time taking my strengths from great to supernova. That takes self-acceptance and self-love.

That said, I think you do have to improve your weaknesses. To a point.

You need to be capable enough. My kind candor was so weak that it created issues with some current and former employees, so I had to improve it. But I don't overstress this point, because most people work only on their weaknesses, not their superpowers. Yes, I want to level set my weaknesses, but I'm more interested in taking my strengths to the moon.

You might not be able to completely punt your weakness as I punted school. You might need to get it to an acceptable baseline, but it's often too much work to go from acceptable to good. Even more often, the juice is not worth the squeeze. I want you to triple down on what you're naturally good at. Ironically, you'll find that it actually compensates for your weaknesses more effectively than trying to turn a weakness into a strength. In other words, the net business outcome is greater when you triple down on those strengths because of time-impact arbitrage.

I needed my kind candor to be at an acceptable level, but I know I will never be the greatest at it. I'll never be as good at it as I am at an ingredient like empathy. Never ever.

If at this exact moment you stop reading and start learning more about self-discovery from other teachers and formats, then this book is the best one I've ever written. That's how much I believe in self-awareness.

ACCOUNTABILITY

The fact or condition of being
accountable; responsibility.[14]

People love to deflect blame from themselves onto other people. The greatest misconception is that avoiding accountability will lead to happiness, when in reality the reverse is true.

"It's my boss's fault I'm not getting paid enough."

"Sally messed up my project."

"That's on Rick for not communicating."

"The market collapsed the day before our launch."

"Well, if the client hadn't made these demands . . . "

When you blame others, you're admitting to yourself that you're no longer in control. You give leverage to the person(s) you're pointing your finger at, and you become a victim of the situation you're in.

Instead of pointing a finger, consider pointing a thumb back at yourself.

"I need to ask my boss for a raise or get a new job."

"I have to set a better framework to work with Sally in the future."

"I need to set up quick check-in meetings with Rick."

"If I hadn't been looking for the gold rush (or if I had moved quicker during the gold rush), this wouldn't have happened."

"If I'd been more up-front with the client, I wouldn't be in this situation."

I think of accountability as the brakes. It stops the momentum of pain that comes from blaming others. If your business partner screws you and you go into a dark spiral of blame, accountability gets you out of it. If you listen to two people arguing, you'll notice that the entire conversational flow changes the second someone takes a step toward accountability.

No matter what challenge I'm facing, I have to accept that in some way I made a decision that put me in that situation. Even if the decision I made was to ignore the situation until this moment, I need to hold myself accountable for that, too. It gives me great calm and comfort to feel that every issue in my life is 100 percent my fault. It excites me to know that nobody else is in control. If I created the issue, then I have the power to fix it. If I didn't create the issue and it's bigger than me or purely circumstantial, I can still decide how I absorb it.

Accountability is the most challenging ingredient for most people, because their self-esteem is predicated on the outcomes of their actions. It's hard to take blame when you're not kind to yourself or optimistic about the future; taking it leaves you completely vulnerable to other people's judgment.

People fear others' opinions, so they develop an ego-defense mechanism against their own mistakes. It's a form of avoidance disguised as a solution.

I cheer for people. I show my admiration for them. However, I don't think others are better than me. I also don't think I'm better than them. When you don't overvalue your own opinion, it's easier to not overvalue the opinions of others. It frees you to be accountable. It's easy to tell the world, "It's my fault," because there's nothing anybody can say about me that can affect my self-esteem.

You might be able to trick certain people by deflecting accountability, but you can't trick those with stronger emotional intelligence than you. People who have a high EQ are typically the most liked or the most successful, and it really sucks if you can't win with that group.

To them, it's obvious when you're passing blame. Unfortunately, many people would rather live their lives tricking other emotionally weak players. They'd rather win with those who are ego-driven and fear-based.

I do have empathy for those who avoid accountability, because for a long time, I also avoided kind candor and one-on-one confrontation. I went too far in the direction of being empathetic and taking accountability for others' weaknesses or mistakes, which meant that some employees didn't realize they also had room for improvement. My avoidance of kind candor always led me to a situation I didn't want to be in. In the short term, I avoided conflict, but throughout my twenty-plus years at VaynerMedia and Wine Library, some employees left because I didn't give proper feedback on how they could grow.

I'm continuing to learn that leaders need to mix kind candor with accountability. Too much accountability can give way to entitlement and resentment down the road for both managers and employees. Perhaps kind candor can make it easier for you to embrace accountability: it means you don't have to passively accept all blame.

If you're having friction with a business partner, you can take accountability for putting yourself in that position but still give feedback to the other person when necessary. You can do both.

Of course, in business, financial stability is the big variable that can make it easier to be accountable. That's why saving money is crucial.

As you work on developing this ingredient, I encourage you to ask yourself this important question: *Can you quit your job tomorrow?*

A lot of people can't. It's one thing if you're twenty-two years old and fresh out of school with no debt, but when you start adding other responsibilities, it's not just about you anymore. Even if you feel that *you* can live in a smaller house without fancy things, maybe you have kids, who each need their own room to study. You might have a significant other who wants a different lifestyle.

Do you feel trapped? If so, a good start toward taking account-ability is looking at your expenses and seeing where you can save money. Can you move an hour away from your office to save on rent, now that more companies accept remote work? Can you sell some things you don't use anymore?

As I get older, I realize how much of my happiness comes from being in control. Financial control is only one aspect of being in con-trol. It's also about being in control of how I use these twelve and a half ingredients.

When you genuinely feel that you're in control, you don't fear the outcome. If you have savings, you can feel safe, because you can take care of yourself. If you're still working toward that security, you can still feel safe in the fact that you can always get another job. There are always more opportunities. The world is abundant, and you're in the driver's seat.

Much of the day-to-day angst people face comes from a feeling of helplessness. Accountability can potentially reverse that.

I wish this book were called *Thirteen*, but it's not. It's called *Twelve and a Half* because I'm still in the process of addressing my kind-candor ingredient. If you know that accountability is one of your halves, I hope you'll begin to do the same right now.

OPTIMISM

Hopefulness and confidence about the future
or the successful outcome of something.[15]

On December 13, 2020, I posted on Instagram a video of a deer skipping across a beach. I gave it this title: "all I want is for you to be as happy as this baby deer . . . that is all."

Visit garyvee.com/fthelion to check it out.

Someone left a comment on that post, saying, "Till that lion comes."

I responded, "And then he will get smart and avoid the lion, too many are scared of the thought of the lion without realizing you're capable of navigating it!!! Fuck the lion."

Optimism is a word that has become controversial in some ways. There's a misconception that it means the same thing as delusion. A stunning percentage of people (probably including the user who left that comment) believe that optimism is just a setup for disappointment and loss. Those who are scared and hurt are afraid of optimism because they don't want to be let down, so they confuse it with naïveté.

Take a second and reread the definition at the beginning of this section.

In contrast, here's the definition of *delusion*: "a false belief or judgment about external reality, held despite incontrovertible evidence to the contrary, occurring especially in mental conditions."[16]

Notice how they're different?

The opposite of optimism would be pessimism. Here's the definition of that: "a tendency to see the worst aspect of things or believe that the worst will happen; a lack of hope or confidence in the future."[17]

Does it make sense that with hope and confidence about the future, you have a higher chance of reaching your desired outcome? I think so. More important, you have far more control of your perspective than you have over the trillions of variables that make navigating the universe so tricky.

Choosing optimism over pessimism is, at the end of the day, wildly practical. It doesn't mean being naïve or blind to the downsides in business or in life. In fact, I'm more aware than most about what could go wrong. I just believe that I'm capable of navigating any challenge. For example, if you think you'll be genuinely happy running your own business, I'm not going to lie to you and say that it's going to be easy. However, I'm excited that you even have the opportunity to try. Your grandfather couldn't start a company on the side with his smartphone. Gratitude can fuel optimism. Do you know how lucky you are?

Optimism is being thrilled about your next at-bat, while acknowledging that you're not guaranteed to hit a home run.

If this is hard for you, ask yourself what your defense mechanism is when something doesn't go as planned. Do you default to blaming others and getting upset? Do you lack accountability? Do you use ego as a shield? Do you crawl into a shell because you're dwelling on the past and beating yourself up? Is your self-esteem entirely influenced by what other people think of you?

Or do you take accountability? Do you deploy gratitude to limit dwelling? Do you have perspective on life as a whole, outside of your business or career? Are you kind to yourself?

The other emotional ingredients will help you deal with losses more effectively, so you won't be let down as often. When you know you won't be let down, optimism comes naturally.

Rewiring your emotions takes time. Start by surrounding yourself with optimistic people, and limit interactions with people who drag you down mentally. Fill your ears with positivity through podcasts and videos—24/7, 365.

Groups who have been historically oppressed tend to draw optimism from other successful people who look like them. That's one of the reasons why representation is so important.

My grandparents would always point to the TV if there was a person on it with a Jewish last name. They'd say, *"Wow, a Jewish person is on TV!"*

They lived under oppression in the Soviet Union. I didn't understand then, but now I see why they were thrilled to see successful people who looked like them—they were a source of hope.

I think of optimism as a map. It helps me see my destination. It's one of the many reasons why I value the journey over the outcome. Optimism makes the journey so much more fun than pessimism. It's exciting to wake up in the morning and play my game when I have hope and confidence in achieving my goals. Optimism makes *playing* the game more enjoyable than *winning* it.

I talk about how I want to buy the New York Jets one day, but I wish you could understand how little I actually care about it. Of course, it would be amazing if it happened, but I'm comfortable if it doesn't happen.

What I'm not comfortable with is not trying.

That's why I believe optimism is a perfect teammate to tenacity. How can you be tenacious if you don't think you can achieve what you're setting out to achieve? How can you put in the necessary work? More important, how can you sustain success once you achieve it?

If I'm climbing a hill and I tell myself I'm not going to be able to make it to the top, it's not as much fun to push through. But if I believe I can, I'll genuinely enjoy the process of climbing—even if naysayers say I can't. I do acknowledge that, much like Darth Vader, you can use pessimism with tenacity to achieve your goals, but it's not sustainable. If you have confidence in a positive outcome, and you pair your optimism with tenacity, success has a better chance to come true and be sustainable.

EMPATHY

The ability to understand and share
the feelings of another.[18]

Let's call out the elephant in the room.

I named my wine project Empathy Wines. In 2019, it was sold to Constellation Brands, but it will always have a special place in my heart and soul.

When I hear the word *empathy* and read its definition, I get emotional. Empathy is a powerful ingredient that has accelerated much of my success in business and life.

Empathy is the reason why I invested my life savings in Facebook and Twitter in the early days. It's why I'm bullish on the future of NFTs (non-fungible tokens, unique digital assets that exist in a variety of industries from digital art to virtual real estate to collectibles, and more). It's why I knew CryptoPunks would grow in popularity, and that rappers like Gunna and DaBaby would have successful careers. It's why I knew the Internet would change my dad's business back when many thought the "information superhighway" was just a fad.

I'll continue to do that over the next several decades of my career. Eventually, I think I'll be looked at as someone who had an uncanny sense of human behavior.

Empathy is my ear to the ground.

It naturally pairs with curiosity, as you'll learn when you get to that section. Curiosity is the work I put in to get educated about NFTs. Empathy is my intuitive feeling that they are going to be a big part of your life in the future. When it comes to NFTs specifically, I get the same feeling I got in the early Web 2.0 era in 2005.

I have empathy for individuals sitting across from me at a conference table, but I also have empathy for the masses. For me, it's as easy to sense the feelings of the person next to me as it is to sense what all of you are feeling as you're reading this book. It's crazy and almost overwhelming to me that I can feel all of you collectively, with all your different nuances, perspectives, and backgrounds. It helps me communicate contextually.

When you're empathetic, you recognize why people behave the way they do.

Why do you think I react with compassion for those who leave hateful comments on my content, not with anger or frustration? If somebody's taking the time to come to my account, consume my content, and then leave a negative comment saying I suck, then that's a reflection on them. They are in enough pain to want to drag me down to their emotional level.

Somebody once commented to a piece of content, "Gary, this is ridiculous, you're not that special."

I replied, "That's not what my mom says."

And after looking through that user's account, I added, "Your photography's remarkable."

I deploy empathy and kindness against hate because I know it takes more strength to be empathetic. From the outside, people think that those who come with negativity and aggression have the advantage in the interaction. I know it's the reverse.

If I were working in a corporation with a toxic boss, I would immediately go to empathy. The boss might look as though he or she is winning on the outside and may trick casual observers into thinking that stepping on others is how you get ahead. But that boss, likely cynical or insecure, is going home and secretly popping pills or drinking to escape. Or hating Mom and Dad and the whole world.

For me, it's simple to deal with those scenarios. I feel bad for the boss. How could I not, when that human being must be in so much pain?

Empathy is the ingredient that provides the answers to the test. When you can feel what another is feeling, you develop an extraordinary ability to manipulate human beings. I believe it's the ultimate superpower. You can create carnage with it, or you can use it to uplift the world, as I'm trying to do for you with this book. I'm trying to inspire you to be happier by developing these ingredients for business success. In reality, this is about much more than just helping you win in business. It's what the world desperately needs.

However, it's one thing to have empathy. It's another thing to use it.

There are mothers, fathers, CEOs, managers, and leaders out there who have the capacity for empathy at the highest levels. Yet they themselves are insecure, so they hold back.

A mother might intuitively feel that her young daughter has entrepreneurial ambitions, but they might live in—say—a remote part of Texas where cheerleading and pageant life is everything. The mother knows her daughter isn't interested in that, but if the mother herself lacks self-esteem, she may subconsciously force her kid to become a cheerleader to avoid judgment from other moms. If you don't have self-awareness (with self-acceptance and self-love, by association), then empathy might be one of your halves. Your own insecurities are like anchors weighing you down and preventing you from truly bringing value to others.

In a business context, my biggest challenge with deploying empathy is balancing it with letting others learn on their own. Two employees on my team had a conflict with each other last week. I know the answers to the situation and what they each should've done, but do I tell them? There are much-needed lessons for both employees, but should I go in heavy-handed and just let them know?

If I do, they might start becoming fear-based. Or I might be just applying a Band-Aid that doesn't create lasting change. They might need to come to those realizations themselves. But withholding feedback can create entitlement. As you'll see in part II, when we dive into real-life business scenarios, I'm always trying to figure out when and how to jump in with feedback.

Empathy is like a cheat code in business and life. I actually think it makes the other eleven and a half ingredients easier to use. You can handle any situation if you can feel the feelings of others involved.

KINDNESS

The quality of being friendly,
generous, and considerate.[19]

At Wine Library, I once had an employee I was really close with steal $250,000 worth of wine.

What would you do in that situation?

People think of kindness as an ingredient to deploy toward people they've disappointed, hurt, upset, or put in a precarious spot. For me, it's about being kind to those who have put *me* in a difficult position. I've been kindest when associates have been rude to me or fucked me over in business and two years later pretended nothing happened.

I often tell my friends with big potential that being kind is easy when it's easy. Being kind when you're under pressure is tough. It's easy to blast off and curse people out when you're feeling stressed. It takes internal strength to be the bigger man or woman, but it's an important trait that can differentiate you from others.

On a daily basis, I rely on kindness to get me through anxious and challenging moments in business. The people closest to me have had the luxury of seeing it. But I'm sad that my aggressive communication style in front of the camera creates some confusion about my obsession with this word.

You don't have full context on anybody else. You don't have 100-percent insight into what's going through their mind or the events in their childhood that molded them into who they are today. So how can you judge them?

By the same token, when other people judge you, how can you take that judgment to heart when they don't have all the context on you? Those who judge themselves harshly tend to judge others harshly too. Those who are kind to themselves tend to be kind to others.

When I first got news that an employee had stolen from us, it felt like a gut punch. I knew that my dad would be resentful of the open, inclusive culture I'd created that (in his mind) enabled one of our own to take advantage of us. Immediately, I went into protection mode.

First, I reminded my dad that people have stolen from us in the past, even when he did have an "iron fist" over the company. It's just the nature of a retail business. Then, I asked myself: "Is that employee OK? Why do this? Is there something I don't know about?"

There was. That person was addicted to pain meds, desperately needed money, and so stole from the company.

Believe it or not, I feel a sense of gratitude and guilt in these situations. I've been so fortunate in my life to not be hurting. How could I not lean into empathy and kindness to find forgiveness for that individual? How could I not feel bad for them?

That doesn't mean you can't hold that person accountable. People confuse the definition of *kindness* with the definition of *pushover*—"a person who is easy to overcome or influence."[20] They're not the same at all.

You can be kind, be candid, and hold your ground all at the same time. When you're in a confrontation with an employee, vendor, or client, kindness will let the other party open up to you in a way that would otherwise never happen. I'm passionate about practicing kindness to create a safe environment when delivering bad news or having difficult conversations.

If you're too empathetic and kind without balancing it with candor, however, you set yourself up for resentment later in life. When you're optimistic about the future, you can be the bigger person when others do wrong by you, but when time starts running out, you start lashing out.

If I hadn't started developing kind candor as an emotional ingredient, resentment would flourish in my old age. I'd deploy the opposite of these ingredients in my eighties and nineties.

Kind candor was always challenging for me because I don't care about what most people care about. I'm not transactional. I'm an emotional giver; therefore, I have a larger capacity to deal with resentment. But at the same time, I know I have to balance that with other ingredients. For you, it might be the opposite—even if you're great at candor, you might be missing the kindness element.

There's a reason why I added the word *kind* in front of *candor*.

How you deliver the medicine matters. One of the reasons many people choose one doctor over another is bedside manner. It's not about only the knowledge of medicine. It's a lot easier to swallow a grape-flavored cough syrup than to drink it raw. It's more fun to be in a humorous, laughing mood before getting a shot than to have tears running down your face. You're still getting the shot.

Don't use candor as an excuse to not be nice.

During the Steve Jobs era, I literally watched nice kids create a harsh, rude management style in their organizations as an ode to Steve. It struck me deeply, and it became one of the reasons why I wanted to talk more about kindness. In fact, it was a catalyst behind this book, and why I wanted to put these twelve and a half ingredients on a pedestal. I wanted to make traits like empathy, kindness, and gratitude cool—just as being a jerk was cool during that era.

I'm not trying to have an argument about whether or not being a tough boss increases productivity and output. I'm just trying to say that, at the end of the day, I believe kindness beats rudeness. I'm sure we can point to many successful organizations that had dark management styles, and I get it. Tough coaches can create successful teams. But if you look underneath the hood, there's a lot more love there than people from the outside realize. There's more context that people have internally.

I don't know all the details around Steve, but I know how the youth in Silicon Valley interpreted it and how it became lore. My intuition is that he had a lot more love and good intentions than his reputation at that point suggested.

Even the toughest coaches in the NBA or NFL have players who love them. Many also speak of the coach being a totally different person behind closed doors than how he or she is perceived by the media.

There's a reason for that.

The concept of kindness as a strength is one of those things that society really struggles with. It's just not the way that trait has been positioned. I intend to push the narrative of kindness as a strength and see what kind of impact I can have.

It genuinely, genuinely works.

TENACITY

The quality or fact of being very
determined; determination.[21]

We live in a world where the word *hustle* has been manipulated and even demonized. To some it means burnout and fatigue, and I'm devastated when anybody wants to associate those words with me.

If you want to be successful in anything, I do believe that tenacity is essential. However, it should never come at the expense of your peace of mind and happiness. Tenacity should never equal burnout. I'm sad that some people haven't been able to separate those two words.

But I have empathy for them. A lot of people view tenacity in the same way I viewed candor. Throughout my life, I've been unable to separate candor from the negative way I saw it deployed in my life, so I avoided it completely.

When I see people confuse hustle or tenacity with burnout, I'm not mad. I get it.

But there's a clear difference between the two: Burnout is physical or mental collapse caused by overwork or stress. Tenacity is determination.

The reason I talk about enjoying the process of achieving your ambitions is that people burn themselves out by chasing a million dollars, a Mercedes-Benz, a Chanel bag, or a private flight. The reason that this commonly leads to burnout is that such people are almost always trying to achieve those things for the approval of others, not for themselves. When you've put yourself in a position to base your happiness on outside validation and on material proxies of success, you will always, and I mean *always*, be on the cusp of burnout. This is why I try to communicate that these can't be the goals we put on a pedestal.

Instead, what if you work on something you genuinely love? What if you work toward a goal truly for yourself, instead of trying to buy something to prove something to someone else?

Being tenacious is about telling yourself, "I enjoy my process so much that I am able to push through what others normally view as obstacles along the way."

For example, in my mid-twenties, some of my former classmates would stop by at my dad's liquor store. These were people who graduated and became doctors, lawyers, or Wall Street professionals. They would buy expensive champagne, I'd walk into the basement and grab it, bring the case back up, ring them up at the register, carry the case out to their car, and put it in the trunk. In their eyes, I remember seeing a mix of pity and ego. I was that kid who was still working at his dad's liquor store.

It was my tenacity and conviction that allowed those moments to motivate me rather than to devastate me. It became a healthy chip on my shoulder.

As you'll see in part II, my immediate reaction to challenging scenarios normally involves a mix of soft traits like empathy, kindness, and gratitude. But as Raghav Haran (my partner on this book) just pointed out as we were writing this, this time in my early twenties was one of the few times in my life when I went with a little more teeth, a little more *ungh*, with tenacity and conviction. But very quickly behind that, I deployed empathy and patience. How could I expect my twenty-five-year-old friends to know how strategic and thoughtful I was at that age?

They didn't know that my obsession at the time was to spend over a decade building up my dad's business as a thank-you to my parents for all they did for me. How could they? That was a rare decision to make in those times and continues to be extremely rare. They didn't know I had a strong grasp of what eighty, ninety, and one hundred years looks like. I had patience and perspective. The thought of working in my dad's liquor store for a few years didn't scare me. I never felt I was "behind" or "off-track." I had to empathize because they didn't know I was going to the greatest heights.

At that point in my life, I had tremendous perspective about time. My thought was that I would make a "deposit" with my time— from the age of twenty-two to thirty-two—for my family. It seemed incredibly easy in a world where I get over ten thousand DMs

(Instagram direct messages) a month from people who are "struggling" because they haven't figured it out at twenty-six.

I found it interesting to hone my craft in the trenches of Wine Library, a retail business where I was interacting with customers for fifteen hours a day. I was sharpening my skills as a communicator because I had to worry about sales every day. The business was our livelihood; it was how we ate. But I also knew that one day, I wouldn't be working there. By building a brand that my dad could leverage in perpetuity, I wouldn't feel sadness in my forties and fifties that his business disappeared after I left. How could anyone understand all that? The point is, it didn't matter if they did. *I* knew it. And that fueled my drive.

Conviction and tenacity work hand in hand. When you have conviction in what you're doing, it's easier to be tenacious.

Throughout the process of writing this book, I've iron-ically been thinking a lot about *competitiveness*, a word that's surprisingly not found often in my content over the last decade. However, I'm realizing that I probably sell short how much tenacity, conviction, and my internal fire to win in my process are foundational to who I actually am. My intuition at this exact moment as I'm writing this tells me that tenacity is the seed to the next book.

CURIOSITY

A strong desire to know or learn something.[22]

I'm struggling to write this section right now because of how excited I'm feeling about NFTs. I can feel the chemicals in my body as I'm sitting in my chair. I genuinely believe that NFTs will create a revolution in human creativity, and I'm so excited to learn more.

After spending the latter months of 2020 focused on Vayner-Media operations, I'm willing to lift my foot off the gas pedal a bit in early 2021 to make more time for research. That might mean my business won't grow as fast, but I can't let this opportunity with NFTs pass. I'll have far bigger regrets if I don't see this through.

When people lack curiosity, they dismiss new opportunities instead of taking the time to explore them. A lot of people thought that playing video games wasn't a practical way to make money. Today, top-earning gamers and e-sports content creators are making millions of dollars every year.

In the early days of social media, many experts dismissed it as a fad. They said the same thing about Web 2.0. When I started talking about the rise of sports cards as an interesting alternative investment, people didn't believe it was practical.

Now, in early 2021, we're at the dawn of an era when artists will be able to generate livable income through NFTs. Yet, many people believe being able to draw isn't a practical skill. There are many passionate, talented artists who are accepting jobs they'll eventually hate, not realizing that they could've made a living doing what they loved as a child. Instead, they'll be going through the motions, working as executives at a bank.

The word *curiosity* is underrated in our society. It feels fluffy, academic, and childish, but I believe it's one of the most important characteristics for success in business.

In the wine world, my curiosity manifested in reading every post on Mark Squires' Wine Bulletin Board in the mid- to late nineties. Through empathy and curiosity, which I think are foundational ingredients to my intuition, I felt that Australian and Spanish wines would rise in popularity, based on the info I'd gathered. And I was crazy right.

In a way, it's similar to what an A&R rep (artists-and-repertoire representative) from the music industry does. My curiosity led me to putting in work to learn (like going to clubs to discover artists, as A&R people did in the seventies and eighties), and then I used empathy to pick what was going to be hot, betting on artists who'd go on to build big bands. That's essentially what I do for a living.

Curiosity mixed with empathy can lead to intuition. Then, after experiencing or "tasting" that intuition, you can develop conviction.

My curiosity ultimately led to my belief that sports cards would explode in value in certain categories. Same with NFTs.

I'm an anthropologist by nature. I watch. I deeply observe human behavior, which leads to what some consider predictions about emerging technologies and industries. In reality, I'm not making predictions. I'm just paying closer attention to what the market is already doing and executing faster than most.

When you have curiosity, you need to protect it with humility at all costs. I don't put my successes on a pedestal in my head because doing so would undermine my curiosity. It would trick me into thinking I don't have much left to accomplish. In my mind, I'm still young. I'm still just getting started. I'm still "in the dirt." If you have an inflated ego, curiosity gets suppressed.

The two words that stand out to me in the definition of *curiosity* are *strong* and *learn*. To maximize the value of curiosity, you need a strong work ethic. You need a strong desire to continue learning, no matter how much you've accomplished.

If more athletes leaned into their curiosity, they would be excited when they retire, not sad. Instead of thinking, *My career is over*, they would think, *Wow! I'm only thirty-five. What else can I do for the next fifty or sixty years of my life?*

Athletes could leverage their talent, reputation, relationships, and knowledge to explore new areas of life—whether building a brand or just becoming a better parent. Players in the Hall of Fame are younger than I am, and I think I'm a baby. Imagine what I think about them—they're so, so early in their careers.

If you're an ambitious person who retired at sixty-five before the era of social media, then curiosity can lead to a brand-new career. If you want to get back on the field, sixty-five to ninety can be like playtime. What if you shared your knowledge from over sixty years of life? What if you could enhance your legacy by communicating to the world on social media, taking advantage of an opportunity you didn't have in the prime of your career?

In addition to optimism, one of the driving forces behind my love for the journey is curiosity. I wonder how big a business I can actually build. I wonder how many people I can have an impact on. I wonder how many will show up to my funeral one day.

I'm fascinated by how big all this can get. I want to see it through.

The second crucial word in the definition above is *learn*.

Those who follow my content on social media are often confused by my perspective on education. I believe education is the foundation of success, but I also think we should question the way it's sold in America today.

If you live and breathe entrepreneurship and truly have potential to be a businessperson, then it's worth debating whether taking on college debt is worth it. More students, parents, and organizations need to reconsider the value of college for their specific ambitions.

That said, the reason I'm on the board of Pencils of Promise is that they build schools in places like Ghana, Laos, and Guatemala. In less-developed countries, school can be the gateway to opportunity in the same way that the Internet and social media are in the United States.

Learning can come in different forms. You can learn by DM-ing someone you admire and asking to work for them. You can learn by going to a class. You can learn by consuming content on Twitter and YouTube, as I'm doing to learn about NFTs. Curiosity is the inspiration for that work ethic.

People who lack curiosity often trick themselves into thinking they're deploying conviction. You might not want to learn about new technologies, platforms, or opportunities because you're "sticking to one thing." I respect it if you don't like to juggle too many balls at once—a lot of people don't—but be careful not to put your past accomplishments on a pedestal or operate from ego and call that conviction.

I don't want to rank the ingredients in this book against one another, but if I were forced to pick, I would put curiosity and humility over conviction and tenacity.

PATIENCE

The capacity to accept or tolerate delay, trouble,
or suffering without getting angry or upset.[23]

When I hear this definition, I smile ear to ear.

My community is probably tired of hearing me talk about patience. But I have terrible news:

I will continue to drill this fucking word into the skull of every person I ever meet. Patience has been such a beautiful gift in my life. Raghav pointed out that he didn't expect to see "tolerate . . . suffering **without getting angry or upset**" in the definition, and I didn't either. I feel a close association with this word and how it's defined.

If heaven is a place where they give you a word on your chest, I know that this will be the one for me. Patience is a core ingredient to the lightness I feel inside. When you have a good relationship with time, the pressure is lifted and you can do so much more. If I have my way one day, patience will be in the K–12 curriculum everywhere.

I wish more parents realized that patience is one of the most important ingredients that children need to develop. We would have much happier children who wouldn't need escapism to cope with the stress that impatience creates. A staggering number of people from eighteen to thirty feel anxiety about their careers because they don't have a good relationship with patience.

I've watched dozens of employees come through companies I've been involved with who seemed destined for great things but were undermined by their impatience. They expected astonishingly high raises, demanded double promotions without results, or made other unrealistic demands to feed their short-term insecurities. They unfortunately derailed their long-term potential within the organization because they were in such a rush and lacked self-awareness.

Insecurity festers without the fertilizer of patience.

When you're desperate to prove something to other people in the short term, you don't give yourself a chance to enjoy the process. When you don't enjoy the process, you become more vulnerable to burnout. If you're forcing yourself down a path just because you *think* you're going to make a million dollars by thirty and you don't, you're setting yourself up for major self-esteem issues at thirty-one.

Worrying about other people's opinions of your accomplishments when you haven't even achieved them yet is a common mistake. Patience allows you to deal with judgment from others in your twenties and beyond. When my financially successful friends came to my dad's liquor store and looked at me with pity, my patience is why I was able to deal with it so effortlessly.

Those who are patient aren't any less ambitious or tenacious. In fact, patience can give you permission to dream bigger.

Let me be very transparent with you: I have not even come close to achieving what I want to achieve. Not even the same realm.

I'm also aware that I've achieved a lot so far in the eyes of others. But to myself? Just like you, I feel there's so much more to be done. At forty-six years old as this book comes out, I'm still patient. I'm not in a rush to realize my dreams in the next few years—I'm excited about the next forty-six.

You can imagine why I try to shake up kids at conferences into understanding that they have the greatest asset: time. For all you twenty-two-year-olds, if I could trade everything to switch places with you, I would.

I also want to remind the sixty-six-year-old that twenty-five more years with modern medicine is plenty of time to achieve what you dreamed about at thirteen, twenty-three, or thirty-three. There's still time to lean into your curiosities. I view patience as foundational not only to the entry-level intern, but also to CEOs, COOs, and senior executives.

When you're patient as a leader, you can give your employees room to grow and develop over time. All of a sudden, you don't get angry at small mistakes they make in their first few weeks on the job. You're more comfortable with training and developing young talent over time. You're more willing to look at their performance in aggregate, rather than overvaluing how they did in week one or week ten. When you're patient with yourself, you can be patient with others.

Like many of the other ingredients, however, patience needs to be balanced with kind candor. By being overly patient, you risk sowing the seeds for resentment. When my patience ran out in the past, it led to murky, sloppy exits. If and when people prove they're incapable of doing the job they were hired for, kind candor needs to come into play.

I have an interesting insight for all of you: Almost every time that I put out content about patience, a stunning amount of the comments say, "Easier said than done." I want to remind you, as you uncover your halves, that all great things should be hard.

CONVICTION

A firmly held belief or opinion.[24]

Why would I go on the public record and write that NFTs are going to create a revolution in human creativity? Why would I put myself in a position where I could be so wrong in front of so many people, when NFTs are still so early?

Stating your convictions out loud is a vulnerability. You might be wrong.

To me, though, conviction is like religion. I'm aware that's a powerful statement, and I'm not trying to ruffle feathers. The reason I say that is because it's a strong belief. I believe in my business convictions like a religion. When I'm convinced about something, nothing can stop me.

Conviction is the north star that keeps you on track, helping you be tenacious throughout your journey, despite the inevitable difficulties. Without conviction, you'll miss big opportunities and lose because of other people's opinions, which is the most devastating of all.

If Elon Musk, Warren Buffet, Oprah Winfrey, and Jeff Bezos all walked into my room right now and said NFTs have no long-term potential, you couldn't imagine how little I'd care about what they have to say. Despite all their business successes and innovations, their subjective opinions wouldn't be able to penetrate my conviction.

But if nobody buys NFTs seven years from now? That data from the market might change my mind. What won't change my mind is the opinions of four people, no matter how successful they may be. Even if they were successful in the past, that's not always a guaranteed indicator of their correctness about the future.

That's why I don't pontificate on subjects I don't know about. I have no opinion on Mars. I have curiosities and hypotheses about virtual reality, but I need more insights from the market before I go on the record with my convictions. I need to "feel" the end consumers' behaviors.

Augmented reality excites me because Pokémon Go already happened. I saw people pull over to the side of the road and jump out of their car to catch a nonexistent Pikachu in the woods. Which means it *did* exist. There's no doubt in my mind that we're going to live in a mixed-reality universe. AR might not be at scale yet, but it's going to happen. It already has.

When I saw nerds talking to each other from their basements in 1994 through this thing called the Internet, I knew it was just a matter of time before the whole world did it. When I saw kids playing Fortnite or buying digital goods, I knew it was just a matter of time before adults started doing it too. In fact, I did see adults do it. It was called Farmville on Facebook in 2010.

I often find my beliefs to be in contrast with reports and official studies. My question is always, *"How'd you get to the results in that report?"*

Is it a true representation of market behavior? Or did you conclude that—say—67 percent of Americans think coffee is delicious because you polled 91 people and claimed the math was significant?

I'm trying to live in constant osmosis with all 328 million people in the United States. I want to feel the pulse of the culture. I'm living in a constant state of curiosity and empathy, which lay the path toward strong convictions.

Because my beliefs come from my intuitions, I don't think I'm "right." I just think I'm old enough to know that my intuition has a strong track record.

I've won that game a lot. People start by telling me "No," which then turns to "Maybe," and eventually turns into "You're such an innovator" or "How did you predict that?"

That's been the foundation for my career. Doing a focus group of a hundred people won't always get you those results.

When you follow your convictions against society's pushback, one of two things will happen: either you'll be right, or you'll be happy you saw it through. If you quit your well-paying law-firm job to start a clothing line and it fails two years in, you don't need to feel ashamed for not keeping your job like your mom told you to.

You can feel relieved that in your eighties and nineties you won't be asking yourself, "What if I'd taken the leap?"

I prefer dying on my own sword over dying on someone else's. I hold on to my convictions until the market tells me I'm wrong. And when I'm wrong, I make adjustments with conviction too.

Over time, I've matured in rounding out my convictions to be more thoughtful. I believed in hard work—for example—and I still do, but now I can paint a more complete picture after seeing how the market has misinterpreted my message about hustle. I've started emphasizing that you need to love your work first, because hard work isn't sustainable without love and passion. I work as hard as anybody I know today, but I had zero work ethic in school because I hated it and it didn't map to my ambitions.

That was me with school, but that might be you with your job. That might even be you with entrepreneurship. Maybe you want to work within a structured system. If you own a business, you take on more pressure than anyone else in your company. Maybe you don't enjoy that. Maybe you want a boss or CEO to worry about the future of the company, so you don't have to. This is where self-awareness can lead to conviction about your ambitions.

HUMILITY

A modest or low view of one's own
importance; humbleness.[25]

I actually hate this definition. Why is humility considered a low view? Fuck that.

I do agree that it's a modest view of oneself. I would argue it's a fair view, even a compassionate one. I have all-time ambitions for my career, but I'm not confused—even when legendary cultural icons (like Prince and David Bowie), celebrities, or influential politicians pass away, we mourn for a period of time but then move on. I recognize how little I really matter in the grand scheme of things, and that's humbling to think about. No matter how many accolades I receive, no matter how much praise people throw on me, I never let myself believe that I'm more special than everyone else.

Humility is a requirement if you want to cultivate a lasting positive reputation and leave an admirable legacy. Leaders can't sustain success without it. That doesn't mean they can't ascend to senior levels and make money. Depending on the organization, leading with ego may land promotions and raises—but those leaders will inevitably be talked about poorly behind their backs. If you want your reputation to endure the test of time, you absolutely need humility.

It's one of the most attractive traits human beings can have.

Let me ask you this question: Would you want to have the people who know you the least think you're the best, and the people who know you the best think you're the worst? I genuinely believe this is a question most people need to ask themselves. Many are confused when they see success stories of people who aren't great human beings. But were they actually successful? How did they feel when they were on top? And more important, how will they feel in their last days?

It would be the greatest devastation of my life if I achieved my financial and professional goals, but the people who knew me the best spoke about me the worst. I never want that legacy. It would crush me.

Because my humility is the least obvious ingredient in my content, I think it's the one that wins over those closest to me. Most people confuse my passion with my ability to have compassion. People who consume my content on social media may think my aggressiveness and competitiveness overshadow my other traits.

We didn't include competitiveness as an ingredient in this book, but it was right on the precipice. If I ever write a sequel with new ingredients, I'm sure it will make it. Or maybe the reason I'm holding it back is that competitiveness may need to be a whole book by itself.

It's funny how I think about competition. I want to bash my competition's collective face in when I'm playing them on the field, but if I lose, I immediately deploy humility. I lost. I can't be delusional. It's the ingredient that allows me to enjoy the merit of business, whether I win or lose.

Humility creates a comforting feeling of safety that can help you move quicker in business. If I lose everything, I'm humble enough to live in a cheaper apartment. I'm not joking when I say I could literally live in a box in Kansas. I would wake up, use my charisma and work ethic to shower for free somewhere, and start all over. I can downsize my lifestyle without taking an ego hit, so I'm not scared to take calculated risks in business. My humility keeps me safe at all times.

What are people going to say? That they can't believe I dropped so much? That they saw it coming? That everybody who believed in me got fooled?

If I were forced to live in a shitty apartment due to a financial situation, I would take full accountability. Clearly there was a flaw in my operating system that led to catastrophically bad behavior and a series of mistakes. With humility and the self-love that comes with self-awareness, it would be easier to take accountability. Of course, I never *want* to be in such a tough situation, but at the same time, I'm not afraid, because I know how to use these twelve and a half ingredients to respond to every scenario. Humility helps bring out the flavor of many of the other ingredients.

Almost everyone reading this can find ways to spend less money, and yet they don't think so. Downgrading your lifestyle makes it more realistic to follow your passion or take a calculated risk in your career. You don't have much to fear. But for some people making $248,000 a year, the thought of making $200,000 sends shivers down their spines. They're not willing to trade in their car, sell their home, or give up a luxury vacation to live a bit more humbly. You can replace those numbers with $80,000 and $68,000, or with $40,000 and $34,000. It's still the same game.

If you're willing to go backward financially for the short term, you don't need to fear losing your job or shutting down your business after three years. All of a sudden, taking the leap to run your small YouTube channel full-time isn't as scary anymore. You're not fazed by your colleagues looking down on you for quitting your job as an executive to build a vlog around your passion for root beer.

When you have a fair, modest view of yourself, you have a significant advantage over others, because you're willing to do what they aren't. For those of you looking to build your brand, you need humility to post a video of yourself on the Internet for the first time.

Humility keeps you from overthinking the aspects of content creation that slow most people down: *Does my picture look nice enough? What will people think of these colors?*

You can also change your mind more easily when faced with new data. For example, managers and leaders tend to fire bad employees too slowly because they have more pride in being "good at hiring" than in running a good business. If you're humble, you can admit when you misjudged the candidate.

Because of my humility, I don't feel the need to stay consistent with decisions I've made. I can change my opinion in two seconds, and I do it all the time. I'm so hot on my NFT projects right now, but if more important things come along, I'll have zero hesitation in shifting NFTs to a lower priority.

My definition of *humility* would be "a comfort in one's own understanding of one's position in the world." I feel that's more accurate. Fuck you, Oxford English Dictionary. ;)

AMBITION

A strong desire to do or achieve something, typically
requiring determination and hard work.[26]

You know what will happen in eleven years if Sally Thompson
buys the Jets instead of me?

The whole world would make fun of me. Can you imagine what
those social-media posts would look like? I'd get completely shit on.

I've put myself in a position where if I don't pull off that highly
unlikely feat, I'll be considered a failure by the masses. Even if I do
make $2 billion. Even if I become one of the most accomplished
businessmen. If I don't buy the Jets, the world will say I lost.

Strangely, it excites me. Because one of two things will happen:

I'll buy the Jets and create one of the most inspiring life stories ever. Or I won't, which would give me the opportunity to teach the world important lessons through my actions—that you should do it for the journey, not the destination.

No matter what the outcome is, I've already won. Setting a goal to buy the Jets gives me the opportunity to build and grow businesses my whole life, which is what brings me joy. It's so much fun to strategize and put all the pieces together; it's like a big puzzle that I get to solve.

My thirty-year mission is to buy major brands when they're underpriced, grow them, flip them for billions of dollars, and buy the Jets. I built VaynerMedia as a strategic step in that direction. Our work with Fortune 500 brands helps me learn how they operate. I needed to build that foundation so I can use VaynerMedia's capabilities to grow brands I acquire in the future. It could also help in starting new brands, or something I don't even see now, but having VaynerMedia's infrastructure allows me to scale the opportunities of the future.

People tend to have an unhealthy relationship with ambition partly because they use it as a cover-up for their insecurities. Some people set goals to build successful businesses or secure prestigious titles in organizations so they can prove something to their parents, their significant others, or their high school friends who doubted them. Their ambitions are great, but their motivation is based more on insecurity than curiosity or self-awareness.

That's why people set time constraints for their goals. I was never desperate to buy the Jets by my thirties or forties. I was always working toward it for myself, nobody else. I'll be thrilled if I get there in my sixties, seventies, or beyond.

Just as I couldn't separate candor from negativity in the past, and just as some can't separate tenacity from burnout, another group of people aren't able to separate being ambitious from being mean. They see leaders drunk with ambition destroy everything in their path on the way to their goals. It's what I'm trying to change with this book. Winning at all costs has consequences.

Life is a joy when you have good relationships with your ambitions. I wake up every morning and chase my dream, yet I'm so not in need of achieving it. It's a beautiful blend of conviction and humility. I fully believe I'll make it, yet I don't *need* to make it. Ambition is like a healthy "carrot."

Ask yourself what you want to achieve, and more important, why you want to achieve it. Are you telling everybody you're going to own a sports team because you want their respect and admiration? Do you really just want a cushy nine-to-five job and three vacations a year? Do you actually want to deal with the headaches that come with being a CEO? Do you just want to leverage that title on Instagram and LinkedIn?

At the other extreme, are you *afraid* of telling others about your ambition because you fear they'll think you're delusional?

I love talking about my ambition publicly, in front of the world, because it holds me accountable. Doing so also gives the whole world permission to laugh at me if I fail.

But here's where all the ingredients tie in together. Ultimately, I'm not doing it for anybody else but me.

PART II

Real-Life Scenarios

I'm fascinated by how a steak, fish, or salad is entirely at the mercy of the ingredients used to make it. A salad can taste wildly different depending on the type of dressing you use or the mixture of toppings you add. Not using enough salt can make food taste bland, but too much can overpower the other flavors.

Likewise, the ingredients in part I are effective only when they're used in appropriate mixtures. What you're about to read is my perspective on how to use them in combinations to respond to various real-life scenarios, like:

> - negotiating a raise,
> - getting your boss to recognize your efforts,
> - watching your colleague get a promotion over you,
> - confronting a business partner who stole from you,
> - voicing mental health concerns at work,
> - improving your team's enthusiasm, drive, and overall performance,
> - being thrust into a management position unexpectedly,
> - staying ahead of the curve with new innovations, and
> - deciding whether to stay at a job or pursue a side hustle full-time.

And more. Some of these scenarios were inspired by messages from my text community (text 212-931-5731 to sign up). Others were inspired by comments on social media, conversations from real life, or questions I get at keynotes.

As you read how I'd use the twelve and a half ingredients in the following scenarios, I don't want you to blindly think I'm right. By reading my perspective, I want you to develop your own way of using these ingredients in the combinations that are right for you and the scenarios in your life.

———

Scenario 1: You and your coworker Brandon started working at the company around the same time. You believe that you're both pretty similar when it comes to your skill set, personality, and drive. Out of the ten people on your team, you two are the best. However, the promotion slot goes to Brandon, not you. What would you do?

———

The first ingredient that came to mind for me was kindness. I genuinely believe that if you start your reaction by being happy for your coworker, you feel lighter inside. When you feel light inside, the conversation that needs to happen next becomes easier. To get honest feedback, you can set up a meeting with the decision maker (i.e., your manager) and say this:

First of all, Brandon is amazing, and I'm so pumped for his promotion. I respect the decision you made, but I'd like to be educated on how you're thinking about this. What made you choose Brandon?

Regardless of what the answer is, remember that it's not a definitive statement about you. It's one person's subjective opinion when a choice had to be made. It's not a scarlet letter or a final judgment on your capabilities. The manager's making a call based on what he or she is able to "see."

On my personal team, either I or Andy Krainak (who runs my

team) has made a decision on who's good or not good. Even though I'm always watching how my team members are performing and I'm highly intuitive, I'm still missing a large amount of data on my employees. I don't have 100-percent context on what's happening. No manager or leader does. Don't feel bad about yourself just because one or two people subjectively decided that Brandon is better than you at work.

Keeping that in mind, what you *don't* want to do is come into the conversation with guns a-blazing. Anybody who starts the meeting with anger or aggression instead of kind candor has already set the foundation for an unfavorable outcome. It becomes an event that's far more detrimental to one's career than any perceived lack of accomplishments. If you come in hot, it's over before it starts.

As you're reading these scenarios and my suggested reactions, you might be thinking that they're noble but hard to execute. In other words, "easier said than done." If that's you, you have to understand that you're a triggered human being. I have empathy for that; we all have challenges in developing these ingredients. For some, it's more difficult than it is for others. There are people whom I love inside out who would find it impossible to do almost everything I'm suggesting in this book. It just means that your emotional capacity isn't strong enough to handle challenges on initial contact. This weakness comes from a million different things, including both nature and nurture.

If the following scenario reactions feel unnatural for you, deploy self-awareness and take a big step back. If you have to, put the book down, light a candle, and think. Ask yourself if you feel that there might be value in this book. Could this be the way to uncover something that's holding you back in business, or even life? Why did you even pick this book up? As you go through part II, maybe you realize that going to therapy is the best answer for you. Maybe it's having a conversation with kind candor with a parent, or someone in your life who created a framework for insecurity. Maybe it's deploying more accountability— pointing your thumb at yourself instead of your finger at others.

———

Scenario 2: Your manager, Olivia, says she needs to see more proactiveness from you. You're surprised, because from your perspective, you've been putting in extra effort to come up with ideas to improve your team's performance and output. You've been sharing those ideas with other team members consistently. What would you do?

———

When your manager or client gives you unexpected negative feedback, how you deliver the following line determines what will happen next:

Hey, Olivia, can you give me more clarity on your feedback?

I want you to read that line out loud seven times.

Read it like someone who's pessimistic about getting another job. Read it like someone who's resentful or angry. Read it like an egotistical employee who looks down on the manager's skills. Read it like a big spender worried about the payments on a luxury car.

Then, read it like someone who's optimistic about the future. Read it like someone who's humble, curious, and wants to learn more. Read it like someone who doesn't default to blaming other people.

See how different that same line sounds? The emotional ingredients you deploy in this situation can change your tone of questioning and potentially the outcome of the meeting.

A lot of employees in this situation would jump to the assumption that Olivia is sitting in her ivory tower, clueless about what's actually happening with her team. Whether that's true or not, starting with that assumption means you'll react poorly to critical feedback. You're not setting yourself up for a productive discussion. The truth is, you don't know what's going on in Olivia's head. You don't know what's going on in her home. You don't have full context on what's going on behind the scenes.

Instead, you could start with empathy and curiosity. Empathy and curiosity give you a chance to listen to what the manager has to say before you make a decision on what you do next. It sets the tone for a more fruitful one-on-one.

When you're receiving positive or negative feedback, you have to deploy your conviction and keep in mind that the feedback is subjective. You're at the mercy of another human being's opinion about you in the context of this job. One of the reasons I've always loved being an entrepreneur is that the business results are the judge of whether I'm successful or not—not any one human.

However, there are many times when we have to deal with subjective feedback. For example, you see it in boxing matches when there's no knockout. You see it in the Olympics and even the school system where a handful of "judges" can dictate the outcome.

Feedback from a manager or a colleague is often subjective. It's somebody's opinion of your work, and although it may be informed by data, it doesn't necessarily provide the full picture.

When you think about it, that realization is actually liberating. So many employees who receive critical feedback at work end up going home and drinking a bottle of whiskey, smoking a blunt, or dealing with it in other ways—all because one person said, "You're not good at what you do."

That doesn't mean you should ignore feedback, but when you realize that it's just an opinion, you can put it in the proper context. It's not a definitive stamp on your level of talent by any means.

For example, if one person told me I'm bad at tennis, and that person happened to be my dear friend Ryan Harwood, who is clearly much better at tennis than I am, then that makes sense to me. That's black-and-white.

The scenario we're talking about here is not black-and-white.

If you see Olivia as your mentor and she says you're not being proactive enough, then you can make adjustments with optimism. But if you don't see her as a mentor—if you feel that she's motivated by insecurity, ego, or bad intentions—you can take that context into consideration when you hear her feedback.

For example, is she giving you negative feedback right before a raise cycle? Is that because Olivia secretly doesn't want you to make more money? Could she have been feeling anxious one day because she received a mean phone call from her sibling, and now she's overreacting to a small mistake you made? Or even worse, is Olivia dealing with a serious health scare that has changed her behavior recently? Does she extract value from her employees because she knows there are hundreds of others willing to take their places?

Remember, being optimistic doesn't mean being naïve.

By starting with empathy and curiosity, you can get clearer feedback. Then accountability and conviction can help you decide what to do next.

I want people to be more thoughtful. Some reading right now will be ready to quit a job they hate. Others are uncovering deep-seated insecurities, but after confronting them, they're about to start getting promoted for seven straight years.

»»»

Scenario 2 Follow-Up Question:
"From the manager's perspective, what's one thing Olivia can do to get the best performance out of the employee?"

»»»

Deploy gratitude.

As a CEO, I'm very grateful that my employees choose to work for me. People have options, especially in today's world, where remote work has become more acceptable after the year 2020. I'm genuinely flattered when a new hire joins my organization.

People talk about how employees should be grateful to have a job, but it's also true that companies should be grateful to have employees. When companies feel entitled, they build a transactional atmosphere that doesn't give people a reason to stay or do their best work.

———

Scenario 3: You are the founder of a direct-to-consumer kelp noodle company. Although you believe kelp noodles are a popular trend and a healthy alternative to spaghetti, you've gotten very little traction so far. You've worked for seven years, spent your own money on the business (money you saved up from your previous job), but haven't been able to raise any outside capital. You have $13,000 in the bank after starting with $216,000. What would you do?

———

This is the scenario new entrepreneurs worry about. What if you spend years trying to launch a new business but you wake up on April 19 distressed and almost broke?

That's the moment you lie in bed muttering, "How the fuck did I get here? I used to have $216,000 in savings. I was doing great. My job was fine, I had time for my friends, and I was fifteen pounds lighter. What did I do? Who did I think I was? Why did I have to start this company?"

It's the beginning of a dark path. People then start beating themselves up and sinking under the weight of past decisions.

Worst of all, they start blaming others, which makes the problem significantly worse. "Why did GaryVee have to tell me to be an entrepreneur? All these fucking people on Instagram . . . Why did my dad push me to do this? Why did my mom not stop me this time?"

People quickly start pointing fingers. But if you're in this scenario, pointing your thumb back at yourself is what will keep you positive that morning of April 19:

I really wanted to see if I could do this. It was ultimately my decision. I'm running out of savings now, but I'm grateful I gave it a shot.

When you're eighty-three years old, you're going to be ecstatic about the seven years you spent building this business. You clearly quit your day job for a reason. If you had stayed and collected that paycheck, you might have more money, but you'd be crushed by the what-if.

The what-if is poison. It's a source of regret and emotional pain in your old age. As soon as you wake up and start going down a bad path, call an audible fast:

No, it's not anybody's fault that I'm down to my last $13,000 from $216,000. I'm grateful. I'm happy I did this, because I'm not going to feel regret in my old age.

People always debate over what the "right" decision is in a situation like this. Should you lean into humility and go back to your day job? Or should you stick to your conviction and keep trying until your savings run to $0? Let's play it out together.

OPTION 1: You decide to go back to your day job in law, a field that doesn't excite you.

OK, so you want to stack up some more savings.

When you step back into the office, you'll have to deploy a crazy dose of humility. You'll have to talk to that work friend who made a snarky comment that your business would fail. You'll have to admit your friend was right. Your mom might have never come out and said it, but you know she was never on board with the idea either. You'll have to talk to her too.

Let's make option 1 even tougher: nineteen months after you went back to your day job, kelp noodles spiked in popularity after a few famous YouTube influencers made videos about them, and a major health report came out that caught America's attention. Suddenly, your number-three competitor, who was lagging behind you, ends up dominating market share. You watch Kraft Foods buy your competitor's company for $200 million.

If you choose option 1 and this happens, you'd need humility and gratitude to protect yourself against dwelling and self-criticism. You needed to give this opportunity a shot. Even though you didn't win, you got to try for seven years—so much more than most people ever get.

Alternatively, option 1 could play out the opposite way. Kelp noodles may never become mainstream. Your competitors may also fail. You may go back to your law-firm job, build your savings back up, and meet a new lifelong friend at the company. Maybe your friend invites you to an event where you meet your future spouse or a fellow parent whose child becomes your child's best friend.

Success in business is just one part of life. What if your kelp noodle company failed, but your personal life actually improved?

You can't predict the events that give you the best overall outcome in life. That's why I love leaning into optimism. Even if I missed out on a huge investment opportunity, who knows what would've happened if I'd gotten it? What if getting that opportunity meant I would have to fly across the world to give a conference, and on the way my plane crashed, and I died? What if I actually avoided a catastrophe because I missed out on a deal?

In January 2020, we all got the devastating news that Kobe Bryant and eight other people had died in a helicopter crash. If America's COVID-19 lockdowns had started in January 2020 instead of March, would they still be alive today? Imagine, that tragic event might never have happened.

That's how I think about it. You don't know if an event is "good" or "bad" because you never know the alternative. Quitting your business might have led you to something incredible (like a lifelong friendship) or helped you avoid something horrible (like an accident or a disease). I prefer to look at life through the lens of optimism.

> **OPTION 2:** You stick with your kelp noodle company until your savings completely run out.

Going to zero is a very lonely feeling. Countless people have gone to Atlantic City or Las Vegas with $400, got down to $80, dreamed of turning that $80 back to $400, went to zero, and had to borrow money from their friends to get a cab.

In this scenario, your last $13,000 in savings will likely end up going to zero.

But I'm asking you: When you're seventy-one, will you feel better about yourself for going all the way to zero before going back to your law-firm job, or will you feel better about saving that $13,000?

Cutting your losses is important, but limiting regret is important too. Even if kelp noodles never become mainstream, your competitors never explode in growth, and Kraft Foods never makes a $200 million acquisition in the space, you can feel proud at seventy-one that you left it all on the field.

There is no right decision here, which depends on your own goals in this scenario, but here's my ultimate point:

If you look at every decision you make through the lens of optimism and layer it with kindness to yourself, there's almost never a wrong decision. If you look at it through pessimism, there are problems with every decision. That's why I'm always happy in the grand scheme of things.

>»»

"My natural instinct is to be pessimistic rather than optimistic. How do I fix that?"

>»»

By hanging out with optimistic people. The more time you spend with practical, optimistic people, the more you'll shift your mind-set.

———

Scenario 4: You're a mother of two children who had a lot of ambition early in your career. After having children, you happily decided to be a stay-at-home mom. One day, your grandmother passes away, at ninety-three, after living a long, fulfilling life. You always admired her, and you launch a blueberry-jam company as a side hustle inspired by her homemade recipes from your childhood. The business exploded in growth in its first year, but you're trying to balance that with raising your two kids, currently twelve and five years old. What do you do?

———

Self-awareness comes first. Where do you want to take the business? Do you want to sell it? Bring in a partner? Continue growing it to millions of dollars a year?

Then you absolutely need to be kind to yourself. As a stay-at-home mom, you've been the CEO of the household. Now that you're also the CEO of a company, the likelihood of dropping balls is high.

You might be seven minutes late when picking up your five-year-old son from soccer practice, when you're normally on time. You might have enough time to sign up your five-year-old for only one extracurricular when your twelve-year-old was part of three. You might feel guilty because you can't spend as much time helping your twelve-year-old with homework because you have to pack ship-ments, and now she's getting a C in science for the first time after being a straight-A student.

You'll also receive judgment from other parents, maybe even your own. Your mom might say that you need to focus more on your kids (her grandkids) and ditch your business. Maybe your mom sacri-ficed her entrepreneurial aspirations to take care of you, and now she expects you to do the same for your kids.

One way to react is to say, "I *am* going to shut this jam business down. I'll do it when the kids are done with school."

If that's genuinely what you want to do and what makes you happy, then that's a perfectly fine decision. However, a lot of moms in this scenario shut their businesses down out of guilt. Over time, they'll develop something much worse: resentment.

Resentment builds up when you suppress your own happiness for the sake of others. Shutting down your business so your daughter can get an A in science might lead to conscious or subconscious resentment of her or the people who pushed you into that decision.

Instead, consider looking at the situation through an optimistic lens. You don't realize that your daughter is watching your every move as you're running your business. Through your actions, you're inspiring a young girl who will one day believe she can become president of the United States if she wants to. You're teaching her patience and ambition. Other moms might judge you for letting your daughter get a C in science, but you're setting her up to win at life.

You need to be kind to yourself to keep external judgment from getting to you mentally. Day-to-day losses will happen frequently in this scenario.

Here's another challenge you may deal with: Your twelve-year-old daughter frantically calls you on a Friday night from a sleepover. She wants to come home because some of the other girls are picking on her and pressuring her to drink alcohol.

You think, *Oh shit, I'm packing all my items tonight and I need to ship them out tomorrow, so customers get the orders in time for their events.*

But it's your daughter, so you stop packing and drive over immediately. When you get back home, she wants to sit down and talk, and you want to be there for her. You don't get your packing done, and you ship your blueberry-jam orders out on Monday instead.

On Friday of that week, you get e-mails, calls, and messages on social media from customers who want refunds. Since you sent the shipments two days late, some of the orders didn't arrive on time for their event.

In this example, you beautifully chose to support your daughter instead of supporting your business. But that was your decision. Don't lie there on Friday night and start blaming your husband for not helping you pack boxes. Don't blame any of your customers for not supporting you, even if some of them happen to be good friends of yours.

When people are hurting on the inside, they lash out by blaming others. They desperately look for a coping mechanism, which usually comes in the form of pointing fingers.

It might not seem like it at first, but accountability is the cure. "I made that decision."

You also need patience. "This is one bad day in the grand scheme of a fifty-plus-year business. It doesn't mean anything."

And conviction. "I'm still going to build one of the greatest blueberry-jam businesses of all time."

And especially gratitude. Take a step back here and realize that your daughter was being bullied and peer-pressured to drink. That night could've ended terribly. Imagine if she died of alcohol poisoning, and you found out on a panicked four a.m. phone call from the sleepover host's dad. You would've been able to spend Friday night packing boxes to get the orders sent on Saturday. But at what cost?

When you scare yourself into having perspective, you can put your problems in their appropriate context. It doesn't feel good to get refund requests from customers when you've spent hours making your blueberry jam, but how does that challenge rank in comparison to everything else that could've gone wrong that night?

I know in these scenarios I've used some pretty aggressive examples as what-ifs, like me dying in a plane crash on the way to a conference or your daughter dying of alcohol poisoning. They may seem too extreme and unlikely, but these are things that actually happen in the world. I find that most of us dwell on stuff that ultimately doesn't matter because we lose the context of how lucky we are when these extreme events don't happen. I apologize that I've been aggressive so far, but I will continue to be this way because it's my truth.

»»»

"It's tough to feel gratitude when you're in the heat of the moment. How do you do that?"

»»»

Many people misunderstand gratitude. They think you should be grateful for material things—a nice car, a mansion, a fancy watch.

Gratitude is best when it's grounded in simplicity. I'm grateful that the people closest to me are healthy and alive. Naturally, I'm happy every day. All I truly care about is that one thing. Everything else is secondary.

»»»

"How can a stay-at-home parent overcome judgment from others when starting a business?"

»»»

A stay-at-home mom might hear the following statement from her mother: "I had so many business ideas, but I didn't pursue them because I wanted to make time for you."

There's a lot of context missing. Maybe her mother had a spouse with a high income, so she didn't have to work. Maybe her mother didn't have strong business aspirations, didn't have a strong entrepreneurial itch.

People who judge you or compare your situation to theirs don't have all the context. There are a million variables in play.

———

Scenario 5: You're a student at one of the best business schools in the world. You have a high GPA, run a couple of student organizations, and are well positioned to get lucrative job offers. Most of your fellow students are interviewing at investment banks, management consulting firms, or Silicon Valley tech companies. You believe that you could land those jobs too, but after setting up an e-commerce store last summer, you're fascinated by the idea of selling your own hoodies full-time. Your online store is currently bringing in only about $5,000 per year on the side, and you've got $61,000 in student loan debt. What would you do?

———

If you're going to make this jump, the first thing you have to realize is that the world is going to tell you, "No!" You're going to feel pressure from your parents and friends, who may be coming from a good place. People will look at the last three, five, ten, or thirteen years of your life and say that you're "throwing it all away"—not maximizing the investment in your degree.

The reason I keep talking about redefining success is that I think we're approaching the dawn of the era when people actually believe what I'm saying. Which is, it's much more fun to make $130,000 a year and be happy than make $470,000 a year and be miserable.

If you're going to make the jump to run your hoodie business full-time, you're going to need a large dose of optimism. You would need to believe that in thirteen years you're going to achieve a better money-to-happiness ratio than you'd achieve as an SVP at a bank.

From there, you'll need to pair tenacity with conviction to get through all the booing. It's kind of like going for it on fourth down in a critical playoff game on home field. If you don't convert, eighty thousand people will boo you.

Do you have the stomach for that? There's no doubt that you'll get booed if you follow this path, but conviction along with tenacity can carry you through.

You'll also need patience. It's going to take many exciting years for your store to go from $5,000 a year on the side to a place where you won't feel anxiety on a $61,000 loan. I say exciting because I knew that going into my family business in my early twenties wasn't going to allow me to accelerate as fast as my other twenty-something friends.

I had to have patience, tenacity, and conviction in those days. I really wish I'd had a vlog back then. I wish everyone could see all the mundane work I did just waking up and being at a liquor store for fifteen hours a day every day. I was stocking shelves, building an e-mail list, saving money, and doing actual work.

People think that fast money is the answer. It's the greatest trick of life. Freedom comes in either extreme wealth or extreme perspective. Extreme wealth is extremely rare, and even then, many find that destination to be less of a cure-all than they had imagined. Extreme perspective is truly liberating.

———

Scenario 6: You're a fitness influencer who started creating content on Instagram early. You were able to quickly grow to a million engaged followers and build a community. You then started a successful business selling protein supplements and workout apparel. However, as the platform matured from 2015 to 2021, your growth has stagnated, and sales have declined for six straight years. You passed 1.0 million followers quickly, but six years later you're only at 1.7 million.

———

During the seven-year period from 2015 to 2021, we all observed the following changes:

1. The explosive growth in podcast listeners.
2. The increased maturity of the direct-to-consumer space.
3. The mass advancement of influencer marketing.
4. The emergence of new platforms, like TikTok and Clubhouse.

In 2015, a person with a million followers on Instagram had one of the highest forms of leverage in modern society. If you were in that position, you could've easily leveraged those followers to develop new business connections or directed followers to your different channels to build those up. You could've used that following to build an ecosystem on YouTube or TikTok. You could've built a following on Clubhouse early.

This sounds like a story of complacency, which is why accountability and humility are the two important ingredients to deploy.

If you have ambition to grow, you'll have to eat some humble pie in this situation. From 2015 to 2021, while your business stagnated, you probably watched others grow from 50k to 5.2 million followers because they strategized more effectively, executed more consistently, or had more talent.

If you've been kind to others on your way up, then this is where that karma can come back to help you. When people are at their peak, they unfortunately tend to be unkind or indifferent to others. But as the saying goes, the people you meet on the way up are the same ones you see on your way down. If that influencer who built an audience of 50k up to 5.2 million remembered your kindness back in the beginning, then maybe that friendship could turn into a partnership.

Accountability and humility can help limit your frustration, anger, and disappointment. If you're aware of your weaknesses and recognize that you're not that special to begin with, then you're not stunned when other influencers start outperforming you. When you accept that *you* made the decision to not diversify your following across social platforms, there's no one else to blame. You made the decision to be one-dimensional with Instagram. You're in control, and you have the opportunity to change the course of your business from 2021 to 2027.

In this scenario, accountability can lead to optimism and kindness toward yourself. Sure, your business declined, but you still pulled off an incredible feat. Very few influencers ever reach a million followers on Instagram and build a business on the back of it. You've accomplished more than the vast majority of people on Earth.

Moreover, if you did it once, you can do it again.

Sometimes the perfect platform for your creative strength comes along at the right time. Maybe you're a model and it came naturally to you to pose in a bikini or show off your six-pack abs. Instagram was a visual-centric platform that over-indexed for models and fitness experts because they could show off their bodies and fitness results. That might have led to your rapid growth to one million followers on Instagram. But YouTube, TikTok, and Clubhouse require a technical skill set in your craft. In fitness, that might mean sharing your knowledge on topics like fascia, protein, or omega-3 supplements.

You can still grow on those platforms, but it might take a different content strategy. You could deploy your humility and, even if you're thirty-seven now, educate yourself on the technical aspects of health and wellness so you can reboot your brand in fifteen months. Maybe you could reinvent yourself as a B2B fitness guru and charge companies $10k per month for a coaching program that all their employees can access.

Most of all, you need to lean into your self-awareness and ambition. I made the assumption that this scenario was a story of complacency, but maybe it was a story of falling in love. Maybe you decided to spend the last three or four years building your relationship, and you're fine with spending less time on the business. Maybe you just worked way too hard in the early days to build your social account to a million followers, and you struggled to find balance. Maybe you were too obsessed with buying a Mercedes-Benz, a second home, or a Gucci bag, making you vulnerable to burnout.

I would actually argue that many people are happier with a slow-growing, sustainable business. It can create a more harmonious work-life balance if you can maintain the business size while living your life. You might be happier accepting your current lifestyle, without aspiring for a bigger house up the hill.

However, you may not realize this if you're not full mentally or emotionally. You see other businesses growing, and you feel you're lagging behind what you should've achieved at your age. That's where humility and self-awareness come in. You don't want what other people want. So why do you care what they have?

Take a massive step back and think about what it was that slowed down your growth. Did you misplay a chess move somewhere? Or was it something out of your control for a personal reason? Either way, it's OK.

If it's your fault, great. You can be accountable, optimistic, and kind to yourself. You can pivot and reinvent your business.

If it's out of your control, great. You can still focus kindness on yourself. You had to slow down for a personal reason. Don't listen to other, "successful" influencers or personalities who judge you for that. They don't have all the context, and they have different ambitions than you. No matter what the reason is, there's no solution that involves beating yourself up.

»»»

Scenario 6 Follow-Up Question:
"How do you go from being an Instagram fitness model to a business owner?"

»»»

This is a challenging transition for many for an obvious reason: it's hard to go from being a horse to being a penguin.

There's nothing similar about them. They're ridiculously different.

Some influencers who start out as personalities or models actually do turn out to be great businesspeople. Others aren't so good at it. It takes a level of talent and passion that many influencers don't have, but because entrepreneurship has been so glorified, every influencer wants to be a CEO or a COO.

If you're struggling with business, you may need the humility to say, "Hey, I crushed it as an Instagram fitness model, but I really don't have the passion for advertising or operations. I need a business partner."

If you can deploy self-awareness, humility, and optimism, you can find yourself a partner, to whom you can give 5 to 49 percent equity. Self-awareness and humility can lead you to making that decision, while optimism helps you trust that person after vetting him or her.

You'll be far happier because you will no longer have to work in Excel spreadsheets or build out infrastructure for shipping logistics. Your partner can handle that, and you can just be a personality, posing for photos and publishing content.

Furthermore, owning 50 percent of a business that makes $2 million a year is better than owning 100 percent of a business that's making $300,000 and declining.

———

Scenario 7: Your wife met a woman at a new mother's group who eventually became her best friend. The friend invites you and your wife out to a double date. You haven't been out that often since the new baby, so you're excited to get out of the house. However, you're a little nervous because you've never met this couple before. When you sit down at dinner, your wife's friend and her husband start talking about NFTs. You have no idea what they are. What do you do?

———

Ask! Lean into humility. Don't dismiss them as a nerd couple talking about something weird or assume that NFTs are a scam because you don't understand them. Even if you're not interested, be kind by listening and not changing the subject. Don't overstate your premature beliefs.

Curiosity is the single biggest unlock for you in this situation. You could go home and go on Wikipedia and Google and do some real homework on this. Many people have heard friends, colleagues, or acquaintances talking about something new that could've been the biggest breakthrough in their professional life, but their ego stopped them from spending the ten or twenty hours to get a bit more educated. In today's world, Google alone can get you far.

This is exactly what I did with NFTs. I watched a bunch of YouTube videos and followed a handful of people on Twitter, and I knew enough to be dangerous within a week. That knowledge is going to be the foundation for some big NFT projects.

That's curiosity.

If you go home from that dinner and Google NFTs, watch fifty YouTube videos, and follow fifty people on Twitter, you might be on the verge of changing your life in a week or two. I've done this. For the record, I've been that person at dinner talking about something new many times:

Sports cards. Dismissed by friends and acquaintances.

Startups. Dismissed by friends and acquaintances.

The Internet. Dismissed by friends and acquaintances.

All of whom looked at me later with admiration but, more important, regret.

Curiosity is a rare ingredient but maybe the most powerful of them all when deployed with a dose of humility on the front and the back. Here's what that looks like:

Have the humility up-front to stay curious and not divert the convo when you hear something you don't know about. Then, be curious enough to learn more. Add some more humility to put in twenty-plus hours learning, not two minutes.

One of the things that irks me the most is people saying "I don't have time" when I ask them to try something new. I have found that people who claim their "time is valuable" actually have the least-valuable time. I've been humbled even at high levels of success with how much more I can do with my time, even though it's a finite resource. Innovation is based on curiosity.

In addition to curiosity and humility, layer on patience and conviction. Innovations take time. I'm learning about NFTs in 2021, but I don't expect this category to truly materialize for another decade.

———

Scenario 8: The upper management at your company noticed your tenacity and potential, so they promoted you to a managerial position where you have to lead a small team. One of your new employees, George, is more than fifteen years older than you. He's been working at the company longer than you have. From your initial interactions, you can tell that George doesn't have confidence in your ability as a manager and believes that he's better at making decisions than you are. What would you do?

———

New managers typically deal with this situation by going out with their friends, popping bottles, celebrating the promotion, and making fun of George behind his back. It hurts me. I'm actually getting a little emotional as I think about it now.

If I were in this new managerial position, the first person I would think about is George. It must be so tough for him to watch a newer employee get promoted. How's he feeling? What are his ambitions? How can I get him on my side?

I would be able to lead George easily because I'd deploy empathy, kindness, and humility. I wouldn't try to prove to him, my boss, or my other team members that he's wrong for doubting me. That's what a lot of people do in this situation. Their insecurities surface in the face of doubt, and they become confrontational with George instead of deploying these ingredients.

Either through formal or informal communication, I would let George know that I'm on his side. The best way to communicate depends on your style. You might be the kind of person to sit down with him over a two-hour breakfast to build rapport. For me, it would be through the warmth of my actions.

In my first team meeting as a manager, I would say, "George is right, guys. Let's not forget, he's been here a long time, and his experience matters on this team. I wouldn't be here today without observing some of the subtle things George did. I'm going to lean on him in many areas for his expertise."

If you deliver those lines in a meeting without George knowing they're coming, they can have more impact than any one-on-one meeting. George might think you're just "checking the box" if you only speak with him alone over breakfast.

As I talked this out with Raghav and David Rock (a videographer on my team), their reactions were quite powerful—I could tell from their faces that the reaction I painted above hit a nerve. I believe most books written about management and leadership would have said the right answer is to "sit down with George and address all the issues up-front." But I think the reaction that I just played out is more realistic.

You might be the type of person who prefers to sit down one-on-one and talk with George, which is perfectly fine if that's your style. But what I'm trying to communicate is that business isn't about the black-and-white. It's about the gray—it's nuanced.

Let's make this situation even tougher: let's say the first project I executed as a new manager failed horribly, and George started whispering "I told you so" to everyone else behind my back.

That would get me excited, not deflated. I was very happy that the Kansas City Chiefs beat the Buffalo Bills to go to the Super Bowl in 2021. They were down 9–0 early in that game. That's a scary score to start off with, but Patrick Mahomes was telling the team to calm down. He was saying, "We got this."

That's how I would react as a manager: 9–0? Good. 29–0? Good. 78–0? Good.

Through self-awareness, you will develop a sense for where you sit on the scale of insecurity and confidence. If you're insecure, it's harder to lean into kindness in tough situations. Without confidence, the weight of your own emotional problems is too much to bear, and you default to making fun of George to prop yourself up instead of taking time to empathize with his pain.

———

Scenario 9: You notice that Sally, an employee on your team, has strong potential and talent, but she's not able to perform as well as other team members yet. You're trying to set an example and show her how to do her work properly, but she doesn't seem to get it. What would you do?

———

First, you need to take on accountability as a manager and realize that you're making a mistake. Doing the work for somebody is almost never the right answer. Doing the work for somebody without that person involved is never the right answer. Ever, in the history of time. I don't like using the word *ever*, but it's true. People don't grow when you do all their work for them, especially if they're not included in the process.

My mother washed all my clothes for me when I was young. When I went to college and started living on my own, I literally didn't understand what people were talking about when they asked, "When will you pick up your clothes?"

I didn't even know what a hamper was. I'm serious. I was not even aware of the existence of hampers because, when I was a kid, I would dump all my clothes on the floor and miraculously they would be clean the next day. Also, my immigrant family would never spend money on a hamper. My clean clothes were always folded on a chair.

My mother is an incredible woman who worked her face off as a stay-at-home mom, with no help and no maid her whole life. But it still wasn't helpful in the context of learning how to wash my own clothes.

When you do someone's job without having them as part of it, that person doesn't get a chance to develop his or her skill set. In the scenario above, Sally will never learn how to execute her projects on her own. In addition, the manager will develop resentment, which may lead to Sally getting fired. That's what managers don't realize until it's too late.

Instead of doing the employee's job, tap into self-awareness to map out how you could teach. Teaching is how you empower others to execute. It's the way to scale your talent, so that you don't have to do everything yourself.

First of all, are you even a good teacher to begin with? Or are you tricking yourself into thinking you're a good teacher because your grandfather or aunt was?

Next, take a step back and see how you can navigate from your strengths. For example, my companies have never had significant formal training systems. I prefer to teach through what I call osmosis. In other words, employees build their skills over time through my energy and by working with one another, which helps my organizations move faster. Nevertheless, at the time of writing this book, we *are* building internal training capabilities at VaynerX and VaynerMedia, because we have over a thousand employees. At this size, the free-flowing nature of osmosis doesn't always reach the entire company.

If you're not a good teacher, consider meeting with HR or your manager to work on hiring an external trainer—a vendor, a specialized agency, or a specific person.

Next comes the part where many leaders struggle: giving Sally the freedom to fail. This is where you need to deploy optimism. Optimism leads to trust, which is imperative when you're training people. When you make Sally "earn your trust" instead of giving it to her up-front, she'll move more slowly. Empowering your team members to make decisions is how you scale.

If Sally does happen to fail, deploy accountability and self-awareness. Take the blame and figure out your style of giving feedback. Personally, I like to deliver playful zings and razz people a little when they make mistakes. People laugh, and the point still gets across without coming off as too harsh. If I can tell from the employee's reaction that the razz didn't land, then I might set up some time for a one-on-one conversation to clear things up. I also have to make sure that my razz isn't a reflection of passive-aggressive behavior or resentment that needs to be cleared up with kind candor.

Maybe for your style, setting up a one-on-one convo right away is more authentic, in which case you can deliver feedback with kind candor (something I've been leaning into more and more recently).

Optimism is one of the biggest differentiators between managers who build successful teams and ones who don't. I've listened to some people complain about their employees constantly, but after spending fifteen minutes with them over a cocktail, it's very obvious that their insecurities, fears, and cynical points of view are actually the core issues. Some managers think their employees will leave if they're trained too much. Some fear the ramifications of the mistakes their employees will inevitably make, so they put heavy restrictions on what they can and can't do. Some lead with ego and suppress those under them so that their employees don't become "too" successful and leave. Some managers go even further and assume that their employees are trying to steal from them.

How can you grow your own career as a leader if you're always micromanaging and restricting those under you? You're limiting *your* potential too.

I've always had employees leaving my organization to start competing companies or work for other competitors. My companies still grow like crazy because I don't fear these exits. In fact, I propel employees I adore even further—I give them more leverage in our relationship than I have.

There are plenty of business owners and managers who struggle with scaling because they can't teach. They can't teach because they don't trust. They can't trust because they're inherently cynical and fearful instead of optimistic. Lack of trust leads to managers doing their employees' homework for them, then to resentment and failure.

In many of the scenarios I lay out in this section, you'll note that my default viewpoint is abundance: opportunities are everywhere. If Sally messes up and you take the blame and you get fired, be kind to yourself first. Then lean into conviction and tenacity to find another job, which might even pay more. A few colleagues close to you may have seen how you trusted Sally and took accountability for her mistake. They'll remember you and could be business partners down the road.

Someone's always watching. Developing good karma is practical.

With these twelve and a half ingredients in your spice rack, you can navigate any situation, which means you can always be on the offense. You're in control of how you absorb the situation and respond to it. There's no reason to fear.

———

Scenario 10: A customer e-mails you, sounding disappointed in your product. You cancel your next meeting so you can jump on the phone and talk with the person. You find that the customer actually wasn't dissatisfied at all, that you just misinterpreted the e-mail. You're relieved, but it's throwing off your day. What would you do now?

———

Something similar happened to me yesterday.

I got a text from a couple of people on a creative team at Vayner-Media saying, "Can we talk?"

They've been with me for a long time, so I felt that something was off. I ended a meeting early, FaceTimed them both on the spot, and ended up being five minutes late for the next meeting, which was an important one.

That next meeting was a little less efficient than I wanted it to be. The details of the FaceTime call hovered in my mind for the next two or three hours, until I had a meeting with the team members I wanted to talk to about it. For those two or three hours, my meetings weren't great, because I was in another place mentally. The preoccupation "threw my day off."

Instead of FaceTiming those two people, I could've set up a meeting in the next week or so. But I wanted to know right away, and I took accountability, knowing that it's what I chose to do. In that sense, accountability was a gateway to acceptance. How could I be upset when I made the decision that I wanted to make?

When you choose a customer or an employee over yourself, it's never the wrong idea.

Adding optimism to the mix can also help. Even if your day was thrown off, it's just one day out of so many. You have three hundred–plus days in a year and many years in a long career. Don't judge yourself based on a bad day, a bad week, or even a bad year.

»»»

Scenario 10 Follow-Up Question:

"Is there a way to keep your day on track after an unexpected negative e-mail? How do you prevent your day from being thrown off?"

»»»

One of the reasons I'm not a huge fan of e-mail is that the written word can be misinterpreted. Tone is completely lost in written form. When people read e-mails, their insecurities, pessimism, or optimism can cloud their understanding, and a misunderstanding can throw off the rest of the day. People read written feedback through the filter of where they're at mentally and emotionally.

Throughout this book, I'm trying to help you understand your-self. I'm self-aware enough to know that when one of my employees tells me that something's off, I'm not able to focus on those next few meetings anyway. The quicker I can address the problem, the more efficient my day becomes. It was actually more practical for me to FaceTime those two employees immediately instead of wait-ing a week to have a meeting, even though it did make my next few meetings less productive.

It was still more efficient than the alternative.

Scenario 11: You're a tenacious employee eager to prove your-self in the organization and move up the ranks. However, after a couple of years in, you feel that you want to reduce your work hours and take more time off. You have trouble vocalizing men-tal health concerns to managers, because "burnout" feels like a taboo subject and you might have to take a step back in your ca-reer. In the meantime, your output is getting worse and worse. What would you do?

No matter when you're reading this book, your memory of the COVID-19 years is very fresh.

This situation reared its head often as people were adapting to a remote work environment. Video conferencing and other remote work processes created some remarkable efficiencies, and some employees struggled to adapt. They couldn't go out and grab coffee with a coworker or spend seventeen extra minutes by the watercooler in conversation with a friend.

Although remote work increased productivity for many organizations, I still think that those seventeen-minute convos are important for culture and camaraderie. Unfortunately, employees around the world lost that privilege as their organizations went virtual, and many struggled to find their balance as they worked from home. People found themselves working far more than they used to, and some of them had kids to take care of at the same time. Fatigue and burnout occurred more frequently.

In this scenario, I would deploy two seemingly opposite traits: patience and ambition.

Ambition is a beautiful trait, but like all the other ingredients, it's ineffective when it's out of balance. Patience helps balance ambition.

When you're a young, tenacious employee, you're ambitious by nature. Cultivating patience along with ambition helps you realize that you don't need to get your next big promotion *this* year. You can be a year or two older when you move up to your next role or get your next raise, and you'll still have a fulfilling career.

Patience helps take the pressure off. People put so much pressure on themselves to hit arbitrary timelines. They think they have to be at a certain place in their careers by the time they're twenty-two, thirty, forty, fifty-five, or sixty-five years old. How about being happy instead?

If you work in a company that demonizes you for taking a quarter step back after working hard for a year or two, then you're working in the wrong place.

On the flip side, if an employee gets lazy for a full year or so, that might create enough sustained issues that the manager needs to deliver feedback with kind candor. However, if you get engaged at twenty-seven after two years of slaying it at work and now you need a little more time off to plan your wedding, that should not be frowned upon.

I wish more leaders would look at the whole picture of an employee's performance instead of asking, "What have you done for me lately?" In my organization, people might have periods of time when they work tirelessly and then have periods of time when they're more passive. How many hours you put in at work depends on the serendipity of what you're working on, the stage you're at in your career, what's going on in your personal life, and any number of other factors. Leaders need to be fair when they evaluate their employees' performance. They need to review it in aggregate.

If you're living this scenario and you're afraid that you might get fired or reprimanded for voicing your concerns to your manager, consider getting another job. If you're an ambitious, tenacious individual, chances are you're capable of creating more options for yourself. You might be able to get a job that pays more, or even one that pays less but gives you the work-life balance you're looking for.

By saving money, you can open up even more opportunities. So many employees out there are living paycheck to paycheck because they bought an apartment in DUMBO* or downtown San Francisco based on their current savings and $237k per year salary. Once they handcuff themselves, it's harder to go down to, say, $150k per year and take on less responsibility for a more interesting role.

---

* Down Under Manhattan Bridge Overpass, a trendy neighborhood in Brooklyn

I'm sad that people choose fake luxuries instead of the real luxury, happiness. By living more humbly, you can take a financial step back. You could take a job that pays $8,000 less but gives you more downtime to spend with your family. You could afford to spend a few months or a few years building a side hustle instead of always feeling tired after work.

If a company evaluates your performance and potential entirely on your last at-bat, work somewhere else.

———

Scenario 12: You're working on a team that's constantly short-staffed. You talked to your managers about this, and they keep saying that they'll hire more employees, but none have been hired in the past several months. You're stressed out in your role, and you're thinking about quitting and getting a job at another company for more work-life balance. However, you love the people you work with, and you don't want to add more stress and responsibilities on their plate by quitting or setting strict boundaries on your time. What would you do?

———

For many employees in a short-staffed situation, it's tempting to jump to the conclusion that management genuinely has malicious intentions. The management *could* be subconsciously or consciously taking advantage of all the employees to maximize margin, or it could be a different reason. Maybe they just haven't gotten around to hiring the right people. As a CEO, I've learned over the years that hiring people quickly without thoughtfulness often hurts the team even more. The management team in this scenario might be working behind the scenes to find the right people.

Maybe management is dealing with headaches you don't know about. Perhaps there's a lawsuit from a former employee that's keeping them busy. Maybe two of the people on your team are actually underperforming and need to be trained up before the management team can afford to hire more people. Maybe you're even protecting those two underperforming employees because they're your friends and you don't want to see them get fired, but that's creating the inefficiency.

Employees struggle to have empathy for managers in a situation like this, but an empathetic conversation can uncover the underlying issues. You could schedule a meeting with your boss and say something like, "Hey, we're short-staffed, and it's taking a toll on our team. You and I have discussed this before, but I know I don't have all the context. I don't know everything that's happening in your world. Can you help me understand what's going on?"

Delivering that line with kind candor, curiosity, and empathy instead of frustration could lead to a breakthrough in the conversation.

Depending on how the meeting goes, you could turn in one of two directions:

One, you could decide that you're just going through a rough patch at your job. Just as with your sibling or your significant other, you may have a rocky thirteen months because you got into a fight. Work isn't family, but some coworkers do end up becoming like family, and you might go through three, six, or twelve months when the environment is not ideal. People usually don't take into account the possibility that, if they just stay patient for seven months, the issues could work themselves out. You could be going over a bumpy part of the road to something beautiful.

Two, you have the option of quitting and getting another job. It's nice to love your teammates, but you also have to be accountable to yourself and your family.

The reality is, when you complain about something, you're giving it mental leverage over you. Wouldn't you rather take accountability and put yourself in a position to make a decision about what you'll do next? We live in a culture where so many of us cast blame for enjoyment. We cast blame out of our own insecurities and pain. If you can afford to buy this book instead of pirating it off the Internet for free, that tells me you have the ability to leave a job.

»»»

Scenario 12 Follow-Up Question:
"But what about the coworkers? Would it be right to quit in a situation where the team is short-staffed and stressed?"

»»»

If I'm worn down mentally and emotionally, I'm not going to bring any value to my coworkers anyway.

The greatest gift you can give to someone, in my opinion, is not putting your baggage on their shoulders. The way I see it, quitting your job is actually very admirable in this scenario. You're being kind by getting a different job; now you're not going to bring others down with your resentment and frustration.

Here are the steps I would go through in navigating this situation:

1. **Accountability:** "I'm in control, and I'm capable of making a decision" ➙ Eliminates victim mentality.

2. **Empathy:** "I don't have full context on what's going on" ➙ Prevents you from blaming your boss.

3. **Curiosity and kind candor:** "So, what actually is going on?" ➙ Sets the framework for a productive conversation.

4. **Accountability:** "I can either stay or leave" ➙ Empowers you to make your own decision.

If I do decide to leave, I would have another conversation with my boss with an undertone of kind candor:

I wish you nothing but the best. I know you're going through a challenging time. Unfortunately, I'm in a position where something I think is better for me and my family came along, and I felt it was the right time for me to make that move.

When quitting the job for another opportunity, don't disparage the company on your way out in front of your coworkers. You might have had the luxury of getting another job, but one of your teammates might be in debt and might be insecure about his or her skill set. Instead of making Susan or Rick feel worse for staying there, walk out gracefully.

Scenario 13: You're a young entrepreneur working on building a following around your hobby on social media, but your parents don't believe in what you're doing. You have a track record of starting different projects and not following through, so they think that your current project will turn out the same way. You keep trying to explain to your parents that you're playing for the long term, but they don't seem to get it. What would you do?

––––––––

If I were in this scenario, I would go straight to empathy and accountability.

If you just roll up on your parents and start talking about Ethereum, sports cards, being a professional esports player, or becoming an influencer, you'll sound foreign to them. The concept of becoming a social-media influencer or starting up an e-commerce store is relatively new. It's obvious why most parents struggle with understanding the practicality of those options. They didn't grow up with them.

Regardless of what they say about your dreams and aspirations, your parents love you. It's in their DNA. But just like everybody else, parents are either confident or insecure.

I have empathy for parents because they were also parented. You might be mad at your mom, but have you looked carefully at how your grandma raised her? Have you thought about the insecurities that your mom might have developed in her childhood? And if that made you mad at your grandma, did you think about how *her* parents raised *her*?

Accountability is imperative, because in this scenario, you've taken losses before. That's why this next sentence is something more youngsters need to internalize: Keep your mouth shut.

People tend to spend more time telling everybody how rich and successful they're going to be than actually building their business. If you have a big mouth, you need to be accountable when everybody points a finger at you for your failed cannabis business or clothing line. You set yourself up for it.

For me, the reason I *don't* keep my mouth shut is that I don't need anybody's affirmation. In fact, I'm weirdly excited when the world underestimates my capabilities. But if you're in a mind-set where others' opinions still affect you, then work toward your ambition quietly.

Unfortunately, nine out of ten e-mails and DMs I get from youngsters in this situation are on their parents' payroll. Their mom or dad is subsidizing their lifestyle by paying for rent or a gym membership, or even financially supporting their business. If you can avoid taking even a single dollar from your parents, then you don't need their affirmation to continue building your business. You won't feel the subconscious urge to appease them in the short term.

Stand on your own two feet, and you have all the leverage. You'll have to take the subway instead of Uber, and you might have a shittier apartment, but that's much more fun than being psychologically controlled by your parents.

»»»

Scenario 13 Follow-Up Question:
"I think being upset with my parents is a good motivator. Can't I use it as fuel to prove them wrong later?"

»»»

Many people can have short-term success without deploying these twelve and a half ingredients, or even by deploying their opposites. Insecurity, fear, anger, and hatred are powerful drivers for those who make money in the short term. If you're angry and you want to stick it to the world, you can absolutely use that as fuel.

The question is, will it last? And more important, will you be happy and joyful in the end? These emotional ingredients are the foundation for success that lasts. Anger and insecurity can create short-term boosts, but they'll rarely sustain you. In some cases, they can lead you to a dark place mentally over time.

It's like Star Wars. The dark side has success too, just not as much as the Jedis. Never in the end.

Scenario 14: You're growing a service business. You've been consistently pitching new prospects, and you find that they're always excited at first, but once you mention your price, they typically disappear, and you never hear from them again. You've had clients in the past who were happy to pay your rate and satisfied with your work, but you're not sure how to find them consistently. What would you do?

In this scenario, one of three things has happened:

1. You're dwelling on someone who said no, and you need to move on to other clients.

2. You're not selling with empathy and humility, so your clients don't see what's in it for them.

3. The market has adjusted, and clients are only willing to pay you, say, $100 instead of $200.

Here's where you need to deploy: patience, self-awareness, and conviction.

You have to have the conviction that you're worth $200 per photoshoot, $100 per haircut, or $400 per landscaping service. On that same note, lean into self-awareness and humility to make sure that your conviction isn't grounded in delusion. Do you have the talent to be able to charge that much? Or are you trying to fake it till you make it?

If you're a comedian, I would love to hear you have conviction that you're going to make it on *SNL* and become one of the biggest comedians in the world. At the same time, are you self-aware enough to know if you're funny or not? Do you know whether or not you have foundational talent to make it that far? If not, do you have the humility to admit that you don't?

I, Gary Vaynerchuk, will never make it to the NBA. No matter how much I love basketball, it's just not going to happen. You need the self-awareness to know whether your talent and skill are worth the price you're charging.

»»»

Scenario 14 Follow-Up Question:
"I know I'm worth what I charge, but clients still try to negotiate me down. What do I do?"

»»»

Take accountability. You can always say no.

I've said no over forty times in the last month to speaking engagements that wouldn't pay me the fee that I wanted. I secretly wanted to do a lot of those, but I decided not to take a lower rate due to timing, brand protection, and a number of other factors.

If you're not happy with the price a client is willing to pay, you can always make a counteroffer or decline to work with them.

But here's the most important point: if and when you decide to say yes, act as if they're paying you double.

So many service providers ask for $200, accept $100, and then sulk. They become confrontational with the client, provide a lower-quality service out of resentment, and beat themselves up the whole time for being a bad negotiator. Then their brand gets tarnished because of the substandard work and because nobody likes a sulker. That leads to poor word-of-mouth, which leads to more clients who don't want to pay as much—or don't want your service at all.

If you ask for $200 and agree to $100, think of it as $300. Up until that point, you have permission to go through your emotions, but once you agree to getting paid, all your disappointment, anger, and resentment has to disappear. Replace it with tenacity and optimism. That's the only way you can get back to making $200 in the future.

Gratitude, humility, and kindness are also partners in crime here. If you charge $350 an hour and agree to $300, you're not a loser and the client didn't "get you." Be grateful for $300 an hour, and be kind to yourself. How many people ever get to charge $300 for sixty minutes of their time? That's an insane amount of money!

Deploy humility and appreciate that they paid you anything at all.

———

Scenario 15: You've been working at a company for several years. People around you appreciate your work, but you still feel that you're underpaid. You know that the company is having budget cuts, so you don't want to be insensitive, but you also feel that you deserve more money, given the value you bring. What would you do?

———

I would walk into my boss's office and deliver the following line with kindness and empathy as the undertones:

Hey, I don't want to seem insensitive, and I'm extremely grateful for the opportunity you've given me in this organization. But here's what I think I'm actually worth, and here's why.

Then, the boss can reply with what he or she thinks.

Negotiations don't have to be contentious. You can tell the company what you want in a kind manner, and they can tell you if they see it the same way or not. Then you can deploy accountability, patience, conviction, humility, and gratitude in your response.

If my boss says no, I can either stay and work harder if it's worth it, or I can leave on good terms and get another job that will pay me more. Gratitude and humility would help me absorb the news, then accountability and conviction are the ingredients I'd use to do something about it. I will accomplish 0.0 things by staying and complaining that I didn't get a raise.

What this book will help you with is knowing that you're in control. Your place of employment doesn't owe you shit, other than what the contractual agreement outlined. The company doesn't owe you a 100 percent increase in your salary or a promotion ahead of your manager. Such things are predicated on the value you deliver.

The company's judging you all the time, but you owe it to yourself to judge the company, too. Evaluate management's ability to make smart decisions and judgment calls. If you feel that another company would be a better fit for you, you can move on.

When you resent your job and view it as a jail, you're actually resenting your own life decisions that are keeping you trapped in that job. You're resenting the fact that you bought a house or a car you couldn't afford. You're resenting your own cynicism and insecurities that keep you from trying something new. This isn't the communist Russia that my parents grew up in. Everybody reading this book has options.

»»»

Scenario 15 Follow-Up Question:
"Why would you deploy kindness in a negotiation? Aren't negotiations aggressive?"

»»»

People tend to confuse confrontation with aggression when they're operating from a place of fear. When people negotiate, they fear that they won't get the outcome they want. They're afraid of hearing candor from the other side.

But the reality is, most people already know the truth. Most people know whether the designer sitting to their left is more or less talented than they are. Most people know whether or not the person to the right is working harder.

People know. In many cases, they just don't want to admit the truth and take accountability. That's why complaining is so rampant. It's their coping mechanism for pain. In this book, I'm trying to get you to fall in love with these twelve and a half traits so that instead of complaining, you can take control and *do* shit.

———

Scenario 16: You're starting out on a new career path. To get experience, you messaged a hundred executives on LinkedIn and asked them for an opportunity to intern directly for them. Five of them responded to you and one wants to schedule a call to talk more. You're excited and want to make sure that you bring value and build a relationship. What would you do?

———

Some people take jobs or internships where they can't actually bring value because they want the short-term result—whether that's money or validation. This is where your patience needs to balance out your conviction, tenacity, and ambition.

Let's say the call is with a fashion designer.

During that call, I'd ask questions about what exactly he or she needs help with and use self-awareness to gauge whether I'm the right fit. When you consider a new opportunity, it's not just about the title and the money. You need to first consider whether or not you can actually perform in that role.

If that fashion designer told me that I would have to manage a calendar but I know I struggle with detail-oriented work, I'd deliver these lines with kind candor:

I'm a high-energy dude, but sometimes I miss crossing my t's and dotting my i's. Is it going to be a dealbreaker if I book one of your meetings at the wrong time, or misplace a paper here and there? I just want to be straight up with you that I have a little of that in me. Are you going to be OK in week three when I make a mistake, or would you treat that like The Devil Wears Prada? *It's your business, and I just want to tell you up-front.*

It's not always easy to admit something like that—especially if you spent two full days sending out those initial hundred messages, five more hours following up, and finally got a phone call from someone you admire.

But if I take this job, I know I'm going to mess up a calendar appointment in the first week. I know I'm going to make a wrong entry on an Excel spreadsheet. If you take up an offer to be an administrative assistant when you know you're terrible with details, that will damage your reputation with that fashion designer, and that's worse than being up-front and moving on to another job.

I need to be patient and optimistic enough to know that I can get more opportunities just like this one. If the fashion designer says being detail-oriented is a requirement, then I can be tenacious in sending out more messages to others in the industry. I'm just going to have to put in more work.

People take jobs that they know they can't do because they're insecure about their ability to get more jobs.

In real life, I get DMs like, "But, Gary, I'm burnt out! I've been looking for an internship for five and a half weeks. I finally have one. Easy for you to say that I shouldn't take this opportunity."

On the record, I don't care whether you do or not. To the person reading this sentence, I don't know you and your specific situation. But I do know that if you take a job that you know you can't do just because you're desperate for an offer, then you'll create bigger self-esteem issues in six weeks when you get fired.

People trick themselves by saying, "I'm going to learn to be detail-oriented."

They compromise on their self-awareness with delusional hope. Why accept a job where your performance is entirely predicated on how much you can improve on your weaknesses?

»»»

Scenario 16 Follow-Up Question:
"What if you accepted the job but realized it was a mistake three weeks in? What would you do then?"

»»»

Too many people stay at a job for longer than they want to because they were told by their parents or guidance counselors that it looks "bad on your résumé." That's the biggest horseshit of all time.

If companies ask you about it in the future, you can explain to them that you leaned into your self-awareness to recognize that it wasn't a good fit. You learned three weeks in that you weren't going to bring value, so you had the humility to resign. There's nothing bad about that.

If you feel uncomfortable resigning so soon, if you feel that's not a nice thing to do for the business you're working for, you can ask a few more questions up-front to make sure that your role is in line with your strengths. Get full clarity on what you'd be doing, whom you'd be working with, and what the business is trying to accomplish.

———

Scenario 17: You're running a business with a partner, Bob, fifty-fifty. You've worked with him for a long time and feel you have a sense of who he is. Bob brings a lot of value to the company and his skill set complements yours. He's been working with a bookkeeper to keep the finances in order, and you blindly trust him with that side of the business, while you're focused on driving revenue. However, one day Bob says that he's going to pay himself an extra bonus, so you decide to contact the bookkeeper yourself and see where the finances are at. You notice that he's been taking extra money from the business for months, paying for personal things, vacations, home improvements, and more. What would you do?

———

No joke, the first thing that goes through my mind is, *I deserve this.*

Businesses are run with numbers. I love Bob, and I might initially be disappointed and hurt, but the first ingredient I would use is accountability. I had the ability to reach out to the bookkeeper every day of my life. I could have looked at the numbers anytime, but I didn't.

Accountability is the antidote to anger. Being angry and feeling like a victim are terrible ways to start because they don't create room for a conversation. It's also what most people do. Accountability would help me feel better here, because it's not like I wasn't in control.

At the same time, I wouldn't beat myself up for not checking with the bookkeeper. In this scenario, clearly I'm not the kind of person who's interested in monitoring the day-to-day finances. I was the revenue generator on the offense. Self-awareness would lead to the understanding that I don't enjoy monitoring the numbers, and I trusted a partner who complemented those skills. That's OK.

I'm not going to dwell and tell myself, "I'm an idiot" or "I'm being taken advantage of like a loser."

Believe it or not, I would actually be worried for Bob. I would empathize.

Is his marriage falling apart? Are his kids sick? Is there a midlife crisis going on? Is Bob sick with a terminal illness and he's just trying to enjoy himself? Is there something else I don't know about?

Don't confuse this kind of optimism with naïveté or delusion. Optimism in this scenario doesn't mean naïvely believing that Bob was stealing money for vacations "by accident." It means believing that there's potential to get through this in our relationship. There might be an explanation that makes sense. This could just be a blip on the radar of the character I know. **Whether that turns out to be true or not, starting with that perspective sets the framework for a safe conversation.**

If you react with anger, all you're doing is giving Bob a reason to put his guard up and be defensive. That wouldn't set the foundation for a positive outcome.

But come at him with an opener like this:

Hey, Bob, I'm sure there's an explanation for this. I'm strug-
gling to see it on paper, but we've been working together for
a long time. I don't understand this trip to Cabo, these home
improvement purchases, or these private plane trips. Help me
here. What don't I understand? What am I missing?

That changes everything. By starting with empathy and accountability, you've given your business partner (who's probably in pain)
a sliver of breathing room to break down and come clean to you.

There are many individuals in partnerships who've faced similar indiscretions but have actually gone through with forgiveness.
There are partners who stole money from each other who go on to
have a better partnership after having that discussion. It doesn't
necessarily have to be the end of a relationship. Maybe after talking
it through, I realize that it's OK by me, and I can keep the partnership going.

On the other hand, some people could never get past that and
couldn't continue the partnership. If that's you, that's beyond un-
derstandable. You can have a discussion about letting Bob go, buying him out, asking him to pay the money back, or any number of
moves. Once you've had a safe conversation, you can go back to
accountability and make a decision.

For me, if I decided to look past this, will the relationship ever be
the same? Of course not. Would I keep a closer eye on the finances?
Probably. Could I set up a system that sends me text alerts when
deposits and withdrawals are made? Sure.

This is about putting yourself in a position to make a decision on
your own terms. You don't have to end the partnership just because
you "got taken advantage of" in the eyes of the world. You also

don't have to stay in the partnership and work things out if you can't get past your resentment.

When you're playing your own game, you make the rules. These emotional ingredients put you in control to make a decision that you want to make.

Scenario 18: You're a young buck working at a company your uncle owns. You have two mentors, Charles (your manager) and Sarah (your manager's manager), whom you work closely with and admire. You're part of a seventy-person sales team. On a Monday morning, you walk into the office and find out that both of your mentors have left to start a competing company. Even though they want to hire you, you respectfully decline because you don't want to leave your uncle's company. You're thrust into a leadership position at your job, heading a fifty-eight-person sales team (after twelve left to join the new company), and you're trying to develop an action plan. What would you do?

Start with self-awareness and empathy. Empathy would help you feel what your new team of fifty-eight is feeling. Some people may have wanted to work for Charles and Sarah but weren't asked. Some may have wanted to stay because they enjoy the stability of your uncle's company. Others may have been asked but decided to stay because they're loyal to the organization.

Empathy will help build confidence and inspire the team. It would play a vital role in the next six months or year, when the situation is murky—especially the next six to ten weeks.

Self-awareness can help in understanding how to lead. The mistake most people make when they move into management positions is trying to be like the managers before them. If Charles and Sarah used to run meetings in a free-flowing way but you need more structure, you don't need to copy them. You may not be as charismatic or extroverted. You may not have as much conviction when you communicate. You might stumble over your words a little bit. Despite all that, you can still be a strong leader.

Not every leader needs to be extroverted with high energy. If you lean into self-awareness, humility, and empathy, you can address your differences from the prior leaders up-front.

For example, on that Monday morning, you could call a meeting with the entire team and say something like this:

I know I'm young. As you know, this is my uncle's company, and I've been coming here since I was a kid. I'm as devastated here as anybody else about Charles and Sarah leaving. But now, it's my responsibility and our responsibility to beat them.

It's like sports. Just because they left, it doesn't mean that they're the mortal enemy. It doesn't mean we're fighting to the end. We don't need to gossip and whisper about them or the twelve people who went with them. I don't need to hear rumors over the next three weeks that Johnny from our team texted with someone from the other team.

Teams trade players. Sometimes players leave, and some-

times they sign with different teams. I'm not saying it's fun. If somebody went from the Jets to the Patriots, that's a rivalry. But is it really a problem?

We might be in a rivalry now with Charles and Sarah, but remember, that's only in the context of business. You can still be friends with Karen's husband, John, who left to work for the other company but happens to be your best buddy.

Sure, we want to beat them on the field in business, but let's not make it too dramatic. You can still be friends with any of the people who went over there, including Charles and Sarah.

At the same time, remember, you're wearing our jersey right now. And while you're wearing this jersey, we're trying to slay them and everybody else that competes with us. We don't need to make this political. We don't need to make this weird. But we do need to go out there and sell.

»»»

Scenario 18 Follow-Up Question:
"When thrust into management positions, what skills does one need to develop?"

»»»

Emotional intelligence helps, no matter what you're doing, but it's even more valuable for managers because they affect more people. When you have employees or team members that you're responsible for, your emotional skills and failings are magnified. If you've developed these twelve and a half ingredients or other ingredients you admire, people will notice. If you haven't, people will notice.

You might be better than other managers in technical skills, but if you're not optimistic, you'll face challenges in scaling your team. If you're not empathetic, you'll struggle in getting people on your side. If you're not curious, you won't innovate as quickly.

———

Scenario 19: You work in a big city at a finance job you hate going to every day. You have a family, and it's important for you to have enough income to sustain their lifestyle. Even though you hate your job, it pays the bills. On the side, you've been working on a blog that reviews gelato restaurants in your city, and you're just coming to the point where you have enough money from affiliate revenue to feel comfortable quitting your job. Then, Google hits your site with an algorithm update, and it tanks in revenue. What would you do?

———

If I've relied strictly on Google and haven't built a brand and traffic from social-media content or other avenues (like press or direct mail), then I deserve this. I should've had traffic from channels like LinkedIn, Instagram, TikTok, or others, so I'd take on that accountability.

Next comes optimism.

In this scenario, I've already achieved so many things. I'm making good money at a job in a big city, and I clearly have the ability to build a revenue source of my own. I would be optimistic that what took me a few years to build up on search is something I can build up faster on social media. I would start the process of building a multidimensional traffic generator based on several social-media channels, e-mail, affiliates, and influencers and building my SEO (search-engine optimization) back up.

Self-awareness also plays a big role here. I'm clearly unhappy in this situation. I thought I was almost out of this jail financially. In this scenario, I'm going to have a conversation with my significant other, express how I feel about all this, and maybe I would move out of the big city for a while to reduce my expenses. Where I live might not matter as much, especially after COVID. I would deploy self-awareness and reconsider how much it really matters to me and my family to live in such an expensive location.

That might mean I commute farther to my job and convince the company I work for to let me work remotely and come in a couple of days a week, since COVID has made remote work more acceptable. I could grin and bear a two-hour commute twice a week and put in more work on my side project on the other days with lower lifestyle costs.

Or if I love being in the city, going to restaurants, and being out till one o'clock in the morning, that's OK too. I could continue living in the city with my family and having higher expenses. I would just have to deploy patience and accept the fact that it might take me longer to quit my job.

Scenario 20: You're a sales manager at your company, and your team's been underperforming. For the last three quarters in a row, your team has been in the lowest 25 percent of overall performance in the organization. In this quarter, you've been warned by leadership that if the team doesn't improve, they might have to let you go. What would you do?

I immediately assume that it's my fault. Even if my employees are underperforming, I'm their leader. I'm in control of how I manage and lead those who are working under me. If my team's underperforming, there's only one place to look: the mirror.

Accountability is the trigger that would put me in the driver's seat. Instead of thinking, *I wish I had a smarter team* or *Sally's only winning because she was handed the best talent,* I can proactively start making decisions. I would start by assessing every salesperson I manage. Who are the weak links? Are there any toxic employees? Who are the top performers?

I would set up an off-site meeting with my team and have a deep conversation about what I can do to make the environment better. That means empathizing and taking a step back to get a feel for what drives each individual on my team.

This approach also requires humility. Even at VaynerMedia, I genuinely don't feel that my employees owe me anything. It's my job to put them in a position to succeed. It's my job to prove to them that I care. It's not about being transactional and expecting them to work hard just because they get a paycheck. So what if they get a paycheck? They can get one from any company. That's why I always say that I work for my employees, not the other way around.

In this scenario, maybe I learn that my team is a competitive bunch, and they like competing with one another. Maybe some of them prefer developing a deep camaraderie. What motivates them? What do they want to accomplish in their careers?

There are many directions this conversation could take. For example, I might learn that the top performer on the team is the actual reason the team is underperforming overall. The biggest earner might have a toxic attitude that makes the rest of the employees miserable and dread coming to work every day.

If that's the case, I would give that person feedback with kind candor. If his or her behavior still doesn't change, I'd take a hit and let that person go. That might put my overall results down 50 percent but getting rid of that cancer could lead to the rest of the team bringing back that 50 percent.

There might also be underperformers on the team who need some extra training in sales. I would go back to the basics and make sure everyone understands how to sell, even open leads for them myself to help them improve.

I would lean heavily into curiosity here, because curiosity leads to creative ideas. Clearly, in this scenario, I need an idea to spark the team. These ideas could come from what I learned in my conversations with them. For example, if I learn that my team is competitive, I might create a little game within our crew for them to play against one another. If they want camaraderie, I might set up a dinner party over a video call or at someone's house, so there's a more human connection.

———

Scenario 21: You're working in a strategic role as a manager where you have to do detail-oriented administrative work about 10 to 20 percent of the time. The challenge is, you've realized that you're not organized, and you struggle with that part of the job. You tend to miss e-mails and calendar invites that people send. You don't have the budget to hire an assistant, and you notice that team members under you are getting frustrated with your lack of attention to detail. What would you do?

———

Whether you're an entrepreneur or an employee, you'll likely find yourself in many situations throughout the course of your career where you have to manage communications with those above and below you.

In this particular case, you have a weakness that's creating friction with team members, and your managers are probably noticing too. This is where self-awareness and humility can give others a sense of your good intentions. Those two ingredients make it easier for others to empathize with you.

Self-awareness not only helps you uncover your strengths and weaknesses, but also provides clarity on where you're actually capable of improving. Once you're aware of your weaknesses, humility comes naturally. When you're self-aware and humble, you've laid the foundation to be accountable instead of blaming your team members or dwelling on your mistakes.

Accountability can help you advance up the ranks in any organization. Some people remain stuck in the same role for years and years because their managers think of them as complainers rather than problem solvers, either subconsciously or consciously. When you're accountable, you come to your coworkers and managers with solutions rather than complaints.

If it were I, that's what I'd do first. I would set up a one-on-one meeting with my boss and map out solutions beforehand.

Before the meeting, I'd have a one-on-one with a team member who works under me and say, "Hey, do you have bandwidth to help me with some admin work? Is that something you'd want to do?"

It could be an opportunity for somebody on my team who's underperforming in their current role. By helping me with admin work, that person could bring value in a different capacity that's more in line with his or her strengths and potentially more valuable to the organization as a whole.

Adjusting the roles of people on my team would be far more practical than going to my boss and asking for extra dollars to hire an assistant. Even if I did get approval to hire a personal admin, I'd have to be empathetic to other colleagues at my level who don't have one. That might create larger cultural issues in the organization.

Once I have conversations with two or three team members underneath me and find a way to allocate 10 percent of someone's time to admin work, I'd feel comfortable walking into that meeting with my boss.

»»»

Scenario 21 Follow-Up Question:
"What if your boss doesn't like your solution and says you need to figure it out yourself?"

»»»

OK, so let's assume the boss says, "We can't have one of your employees helping you with your calendar."

My go-to ingredients would be patience and optimism. I can either come up with another idea or just get better at detail work. Maybe I decide I'm close to the "good enough" level, and I want to try to improve. I could also be tenacious and get a job at another company if I decide that I have zero interest in becoming more detail-oriented. I'd be practically optimistic that I could find a job that either pays me more or pays less but has a work environment that's geared more to my strengths.

For example, maybe I could get a job as a car salesman and enjoy my life so much more because I wouldn't be spending 10 or 20 percent of my time doing what I hate and spending the other 80 or 90 percent feeling anxious about that 10 or 20. The funny thing is, going all in on my strengths would lead to higher performance and more happiness, which could ultimately yield more promotions and substantial raises.

———

Scenario 22: **You're a business owner who's consistently been putting out audio, video, and written content on social platforms for the past two months. You've noticed a little bit of follower growth, but you haven't had any customers come in from social media. You're trying to understand whether you're on the right track or not, whether you should keep going or adjust your strategy. What would you do?**

———

I would use every single one of the emotional ingredients in this scenario.

The most significant opportunity on Earth for every human being is communicating to the world through social media. I believe content creation on the twelve to fifteen platforms that hold the most attention is the ultimate gateway for opportunity, whether you're trying to get a new job, grow your business, or run for mayor.

I'm going to throw the whole spice rack at this scenario:

Gratitude: I would be grateful for the opportunity to speak to the world. Ask your grandma what she was able to do to get customers for a business. Or what side hustles she could work on at night after she put the kids to bed or got home from work. We have so much opportunity because of the Internet.

Self-Awareness: I would ask myself, am I putting out content that is in line with my strengths? Maybe you aren't getting traction because you're publishing blog posts when you should be filming yourself. Maybe you're trying to imitate my high-energy video content on social media, but you're introverted and feel awkward on film. You might be a more effective writer. I wish I could write, but I can't. Instead, I use my self-awareness, so I'm sitting in a room right now writing this book through audio with Raghav.

Accountability: It feels really good to know that everything is on you. That means you're in control if you want to fix anything.

Optimism: It's a lot more fun to say "Tomorrow's the day when I make a post that will change the course of my business" instead of the opposite. Telling yourself "I'm never going to make a piece of content that works" is a self-fulfilling prophecy.

Empathy and Humility: I would ask myself, "Why should somebody watch one of my videos? They have other things going on. Who am I?" There are a million videos in your stream. I'm just one person.

Conviction: At the same time, I know I'm the fucking guy. That's why you should listen to me. Conviction is about believing in the content you're creating. It's about believing that you know something others don't know about law, landscaping, wine, or how to play chess.

Kindness: When I'm attempting something new, kindness toward myself is imperative. I'm trying.

Tenacity: It's only been two months. It's clear that I need to stay determined. Nobody breaks through on their first at-bat. Most people don't break through on their first fifty at-bats. Or five hundred. Or even five thousand. In the early days of Wine Library TV, nobody watched. I even had an e-mail newsletter sending out episodes to subscribers, and still nobody wanted to watch. Building a business takes time.

Curiosity: I actually don't think I need curiosity here.

Patience: If you follow my content on social media, you know how much I believe in patience. It complements tenacity. I need to be patient to get through the five hundred to five thousand at-bats.

Ambition: I would ask myself, "Why am I even trying to grow this business in the first place?"

Actually, I just now thought of how I would deploy curiosity:

In business and life, I'm genuinely intrigued. How deep an impact can I have on the world? How much can my business grow? How much admiration can I get? Can my birthday be a national holiday?

It's not about ego; it's genuine curiosity. It's partly what drives my ambition. I can't help but to ask myself, "How big an effect can I have on society?"

This book is called *Twelve and a Half.* In three years, will the next one be *Sixteen and Two-Thirds*? Are there more emotional ingredients to start applying in my life?

I'm curious.

And you're curious too. Will your next post be the one that eventually leads to a show on Netflix?

»»»

Scenario 22 Follow-Up Question:
"What emotional ingredients would you use to analyze what content is working on social media?"

»»»

Self-awareness, then accountability.

If you're self-aware, you're willing to see the truth. From there, you can look at both the black-and-white and the gray.

The black-and-white is the quantitative data. It's how many followers, likes, and comments you're getting from each post.

The gray is the nuance. Are you feeling positive? Are you gaining internal momentum? Do you feel you're onto something?

I use quantitative data for validation. It's how I know I'm growing. But for me, it's secondary.

If I feel I'm onto something, if I like the way I feel, I'm far happier. It's like working out at the gym and eating well. As soon as you start doing it, you know you're on the right track. You can tell by how you feel. That's the gray.

You can always monitor the black-and-white. Are you getting

more muscles? Do you poop more regularly? Over time, you'll see actual results that you can measure.

———

Scenario 23: You've been running your own business for some time now. You genuinely love what you do. The business gave you the revenue you needed to quit your job, and you've enjoyed growing the company. You have ambition to continue scaling the company to a much higher level. However, you wake up one Tuesday morning and you just don't feel like going to work. What would you do?

———

Let's talk about judgment.

I believe all those reading this will nod their heads when I say that people who pass judgment on others aren't dealing with a full deck of information. When you judge someone, you're usually looking at only a few specific behaviors or actions. You don't know that person—and even if you do, you often don't know what's going on in their personal life. You probably haven't spent the years necessary to map out what happened in that particular childhood. You don't have full context. That doesn't mean you shouldn't hold people accountable for their actions through kind candor, but it's not smart to judge them for it.

People who judge others harshly tend to deploy the harshest judgment against themselves and their own actions. We beat ourselves up way too much. To be kind to others, you first need to be kind to yourself.

If I were in this scenario, I would tell myself, "I've been working hard all this time, and I'm just not feeling it today. It's OK if don't crush it this morning."

Many ambitious entrepreneurs would grind through that Tuesday. I'm a big fan of grinding too, and I would lean into self-awareness to gauge whether or not that's the right move on a certain day.

It's like working out. Out of the approximately 320 days a year I work out, I don't really feel like it on about 290 of them, but I know if I can just get through the first five or ten minutes, I'll get into my flow. Recently, after about six years or so of a solid exercise routine, I've been easier on myself and taken a day off now and then when I *really* don't feel like working out. That's been a healthy addition for me.

Maybe you're the kind of person who needs to drag yourself out of bed and push yourself for five or ten minutes before you start enjoying what you do. Or maybe you're at the point where pushing yourself would lead to burnout, and you really just need time off. As long as someone's well-being isn't affected, I actually think more entrepreneurs should give themselves permission to wake up and say, "Hey, I'm going to watch cartoons today."

»»»

Scenario 23 Follow-Up Question:
"At what point does taking time off become laziness?"

»»»

Out of about 250 days that I work in a year (excluding weekends), there are probably 7 to 23 when I think, *Fuck this!*

It could happen for any number of reasons. Occasionally, I get hit with the right pattern of four, five, or six disappointing events all at once. I can take a punch, but if you hit me like Buster Douglas in his prime, I'm going down. That has happened.

On days like that, I deploy gratitude, humility, tenacity, and optimism. Gratitude puts every business problem into perspective: Is my family healthy? Then I've already won. Humility gives me comfort with my position in the world. I need to be humble enough to take the punches. I'm not above that by any means. Gratitude and humility put me in the proper mind-set to absorb stress, while tenacity and optimism help me go on the offense to attack the problem. I also take weekends off, and I'm completely off-grid during vacations. That disconnected time helps create balance.

You always have the option to go to work anyway, even when you're uninterested. Keep in mind, though, that it's not about the hours you put in; it's about what you put in those hours.

For example, let's say you had to deal with sadness in your personal life—your grandma got diagnosed with a terminal illness. You wanted to take some time off, but you tenaciously showed up anyway, despite your emotional pain. In that situation, you risk offloading your own hurt onto your team members. You might be angry, frustrated, or passive aggressive that day, and you could create issues down the road with your staff. What if you snapped and yelled at a colleague for miscommunicating a message? What if an employee wanted to talk about personal issues but you didn't make them feel heard because you were coping with yours?

No matter what, I try to be kind to myself in this scenario so I can be a stronger leader. If that means I take time off, great. If that means I just go through the motions at work and lollygag all day, great. I wouldn't judge myself. For me, it's most important to be kind to everyone I interact with that day, whether that's my vendors, customers, or most important, my employees.

Patience is a secret ingredient here that helps balance ambition. Don't let your ambition put you in a mental space where you over-analyze your output every single day. Focusing on your journey over the course of a year or five or ten years is more valuable than worrying about being lazy on a few days here and there. Maybe you had an ineffective day. Maybe you had an ineffective month. Or maybe something devastating happened that threw your whole year off. The key is being kind and patient with yourself first and being aware of how much more time you have left.

If somebody in your family got diagnosed with an illness and you need to take personal time for that, that's appropriate, not something you should feel guilty about. If you just wake up on a Tuesday morning and decide you don't want to go into your business because it's a gorgeous day outside and you'd rather spend it at the beach, don't judge yourself for that either.

If you find yourself always getting the urge to take time off, then you should assess whether you still enjoy running your business through self-awareness. However, don't overvalue your day-to-day output. Your overall journey is a more accurate reflection of where you're headed.

————

Scenario 24: Let's say you have a small company that you're scaling up and, in that process, you're trying to hire an assistant to manage your calendar. You've gone through five assistants already, and they've all quit or underperformed and been fired after several months. The lack of continuity is making you scale slower than you otherwise would.

———

I'm realizing that I'm far more obsessed with accountability than I thought.

I'm the one who's hiring the assistants, so I would start by understanding that this is all my fault. I can't cast blame or judgment on my employees for not performing well or for not staying around. I need to take a deeper look at my hiring process or how I'm operating as a leader.

It's also important to balance that accountability with optimism. I've tried five assistants, but there are billions of people on Earth. Just because it didn't work out five times doesn't mean that it will never work out or that I'm not capable of getting better at my process.

Still, if five assistants have quit or gotten fired, I need to take a look at my own shortcomings. Maybe I'm not being patient enough in their training process. Maybe there's something I need to fix about my communication style. Maybe I need to be more candid in the interview, so they know what they're getting into. Their reaction could help me make a better judgment call on future hires.

When I'm hiring my sixth assistant, I would lean into humility in those conversations and talk about my shortcomings as a manager, even tell some horror stories from the last five. I could share up-front my perspective about why things failed. Humility would allow me to have much more in-depth, fruitful, and contextual conversations that would help me make a better decision on who's the best fit.

When you react with accountability and humility in this scenario, your losses can actually set you up for a much bigger win down the road. After examining yourself, your shortcomings, and how you can create a better interview process to find your next assistant, you can go back to optimism. I would believe optimistically that my next assistant will stay for six years instead of five months because of what those prior experiences taught me.

————

Scenario 25: You're trying to build your reputation with the leaders in the organization you work for so you can eventually land promotions and move up the ranks. However, in the past several weeks, your coworker Rick has often been stepping on your toes and trying to do your job for you, whether he realizes it or not. It feels as though he's subconsciously trying to take over your job. You're frustrated and feel that his actions will limit your career growth and take away your chance to be noticed by your manager. What would you do?

————

In business and life, people are quick to jump to conclusions.

Here's one example: A lot of people assume that just because someone owns a business, they're killing it. You see Bob the Business Owner's nice house, Mercedes-Benz, and company with thirteen employees, and you assume things are going well for him. You don't see that he's underwater on his car loan, his revenue's declining, and he's barely making the mortgage payments. Bob doesn't post that part on Instagram.

There's little empathy in a world where none of us really know what's going on in one another's lives. Bob's employees might resent him for not giving out raises, but they don't know that he's been putting his own savings into the business just to keep it afloat.

The team might say, "Fuck Bob. He's got a Mercedes."

The reality is, Bob's about to lose his Mercedes.

I don't mean you have to prioritize Bob's well-being over your own, but I do mean that approaching decisions with empathy instead of resentment changes everything. You don't have all the context on your colleagues' lives, so why confront them through negativity?

Going back to the original scenario, it's tempting to assume that Rick has bad intentions. But if you deploy empathy, you realize that Rick is trying hard, just like you. He's trying to do right by his ambitions, his family, and what he thinks he needs to do for his own success. How can you get bent out of shape because somebody's working toward their ambition?

(Sorry to go on a tangent, everybody, but I'm just going to plop this in here because it's where my mind went: I think it's crazy that bosses get mad when employees ask for raises. I know a lot of those bosses. Your employees are *supposed* to ask for raises! They're trying to support themselves and their families. You can always say no if you feel that's the right response.)

This is also where self-awareness plays a key role, along with empathy. Maybe it really is true that Rick is overstepping the boundaries with the wrong intent. Or maybe you're slacking and Rick's trying to cover for you. Maybe your ambition is entirely selfish. Maybe he has bandwidth and he's figuring out how to use that time.

If you're insecure and cynical, you paint a picture in your mind that Rick's trying to ruin you. If you're self-aware and empathetic, you see that he's trying his best, and you can start having conversations with him instead of digging your heels in.

»»»

"What would your conversation with Rick sound like? What would you say?"

»»»

Communicating with a mix of empathy, accountability, self-awareness, and a bit of curiosity would work like a charm in this scenario:

> *I appreciate the tenacity, conviction, and ambition you're coming with, but you're bleeding into my world a little bit. Is there any way we can figure this out? Do you have enough workload? Do you enjoy what you're doing? Do you want to do more of what I'm doing? Is there something I could improve on?*

Maybe after that conversation, I could take a step back and realize that it's an opportunity for me to work on more exciting projects, since Rick can cover some of my current workload. Maybe I decide I need to take on accountability and step up my own performance. I could have a conversation with my manager or with HR if I still feel that he's overstepping.

Many employees in this scenario make the assumption that their managers don't notice what's happening. At VaynerMedia, I've had people walk into my office to complain about a colleague overstepping, and they're surprised to hear me agree that the other person has the wrong intentions. As a manager, I'm watching too.

Scenario 26: You're building a new company with a couple of employees who have known you for a long time. Over the years, they've gotten to like you, your personality, your intent, and your vision of what you're trying to accomplish in the industry. As you hire new employees, they're surprised when they see that the older team is so invested in your relationship with them. You notice the new team making fun of the original team members behind their backs, saying they're "brainwashed" and are "drinking the Kool-Aid." The new employees have talent, so you want to keep them around, but you don't want them to damage the culture. What would you do?

Many organizations create poor work environments for employees. There are unfortunately plenty of CEOs, managers, and leaders who don't use the twelve and a half ingredients in this book (or any of their own). They unintentionally create politics and fear in the workplace out of their own insecurities, so employees use cynicism as a protective measure when joining a new organization.

Humans fear disappointment. People don't want to trust a manager or love their company, only to be let down later. I have empathy for that.

When people join VaynerMedia and see how tight my relationships are with those who have been around for eight, ten, or more years, it's very humbling for me. On very rare occasions when a new employee thinks the older ones are brainwashed, I don't get upset; I actually feel flattered. I'm always humbled in this scenario when I notice it happening at my company once in a blue moon.

Believe it or not, one of the most powerful ingredients I would use here is patience. If my older employees truly love the organization and the environment, then the new ones eventually will too. They're cynical because they don't have all the context yet.

Whether it's seven months or two years, they'll learn there's no "drinking the Kool-Aid." It's just water. It's good for everyone, newcomers included.

»»»

Scenario 26 Follow-Up Question:
"But the new team is making fun of the others for being brainwashed. Doesn't that damage culture? How would you handle that?"

»»»

Writing this book is fun because I can feel the difference in how I'd react to these scenarios now compared to years ago. Now, I have kind candor in my repertoire.

Instead of just letting the situation play out, I can set up one-on-one meetings to help the new team with the crossover. I'd meet with each of them and say:

Hey, I totally get where you're coming from. I've been working with the other guys and gals for years. They know me, and I know them. I hired you so that in a few years, you'll feel the same way about this work environment as they do. Over that period of time, it's my job to show you why "drinking the Kool Aid" doesn't exist here. It's actually just water, and it's delicious and good for you. That responsibility is mine, not yours. If you don't have confidence in me or this organization yet, I fully respect that. But I would ask that you be kind to the others.

In running VaynerMedia and building a personal brand, I deal with this headache in real life. If a new employee had the luxury of great parents or she's inherently optimistic, it's easier for her to trust. Employees like her buy in to my message and VaynerMedia's culture immediately. Others who were let down by their mom, dad, society, or past companies or otherwise had an upbringing that led them to be pessimistic tend to viscerally push against me and my personality. They look at my energy and optimism and think, *He's going to let me down big.*

I always respond with empathy. If you have genuinely good intentions as a CEO—if you're deploying these twelve and a half ingredients—employees who start out cynical will change their opinions. It's incredibly rewarding to earn people's trust, regardless of how much else you've accomplished.

———

Scenario 27: You have two employees, Jim and John. Jim has a way of directly communicating his feedback, and John doesn't like it. John says Jim always speaks to him rudely, while Jim says John needs to have every piece of criticism sugarcoated. Jim was raised to believe it is kinder to deliver criticism swiftly and clearly. Assuming you're their manager, what would you do?

———

When managers face this situation, many get upset because they lack patience. Patience helps in navigating this scenario because solving a disagreement between two people takes time. It may or may not be something that you can resolve in one meeting.

Before I meet with Jim and John, I'll think through what decisions I can make. Maybe I can split them up and put them on different projects. If one of the two is clearly the source of the issue and doesn't correct his behavior even after receiving feedback, then I might consider letting him go. But I'd be optimistic that they just have a difference in perspectives with no malicious intent and it could be worked out.

I'd approach the meeting with optimism, conviction, and an undertone of kind candor:

Look, John and Jim, this is just a moment in time. Even if you've both had issues in every single conversation you've had in the past, we're now in the process of trying to fix it. Now that we're sitting down and talking about it, the disagreements between you both won't last forever. I'm not saying everything will be perfect after this meeting. You might still have problems, but if it happens in three out of thirty-three interactions instead of three out of three, we're winning. I know you didn't start out on the right foot, but that will change.

Think about the way managers would typically respond in this situation. Based on the messages and e-mails I get from my community, I believe many would say, "You two need to figure this out or I'm going to let one of you go."

That's what happens in the business world, and it stuns me that people accept that as the right answer. It's rooted in short-term thinking, impatience, and lack of kindness. Why does it have to be so cold? Why can't managers give a little love to their people for twenty minutes? Why can't managers instill a feeling of safety instead of fear?

Let's say the manager tells John and Jim to figure it out between themselves or one of them gets fired. Now, the issue becomes far worse. Jim might start planning how to outmaneuver John. John might try to protect himself by damaging Jim's reputation behind his back. They'd produce lower-quality output because they're more stressed.

Imagine how much more effective they would be if the manager made them feel a little safer. Instead of navigating company politics, they could focus on their actual jobs.

Remember, this isn't a therapy book. It's a business book. Deploying these twelve and a half ingredients in different mixtures can help you build a more emotionally efficient team and a more profitable company as a result.

Scenario 28: You have a big client you closed that will add a sizable percentage to your company's revenue. You have personal relationships with this client, its people trust you, and your top priority is for this to go extremely well. You put your best team on it. However, Susan, an employee from your team, has a moral objection to working with the company. She tells you that she'd like to opt out of the project. What would you do?

———

I've actually gone through this four or five times in the course of building VaynerMedia. Every time, it's a tricky one.

Empathy first. I'd ask myself, "Would I ever decline the opportunity to work with a client because of the industry it's in or the products it sells?" If the answer's yes, then I have to be empathetic to my employees feeling the same way because of their religious, social, or political beliefs.

In the past, I've made my own subjective calls on whom we work with. We've had some big clients I've passed on because I didn't believe in their products or services. So, I can't be a hypocrite when an employee wants to do the same.

If not—if you blindly think, *Money is money*, and you'll work with anyone—then at least you have a leg to stand on in this scenario. But don't be hypocritical.

Whenever this situation reared its head at VaynerMedia, I sat down with the employee who had that objection and had a fruitful conversation where I explored why he or she felt that way. I'm actually curious what makes them say they want to opt out of the project.

As a leader, you need to figure out if there's a different underlying reason why Susan doesn't want to do it. Is her moral objection a cover-up? Is she actually tired or burnt out? Is she making an excuse? Or is there legitimacy and good intention behind it?

Sit down with Susan in a one-on-one meeting and say, "Hey, tell me more. Show me why you can't work on this. I want to learn and understand why."

Then you'd be at a fork in the road. Either Susan comes to the meeting with a compelling case, or she doesn't. If the conversation is intriguing, you can spend time exploring your own feelings on the subject.

The other outcome is that Susan comes with a weak argument and can't come up with good answers when you poke and prod. Maybe she read a single headline on Twitter and came to a fast judgment that wasn't thoughtful. Maybe she actually just doesn't have bandwidth, and she's covering up. Maybe she doesn't feel confident enough to take it on.

From there, you have to make a different kind of decision: Do you build Susan up? Do you give it a mulligan and let her sit this one out? Is there a bigger issue here that you have to do something about? This is a person's career we're talking about, and you're paying a salary. What should be your next move?

Let's keep playing it out: Suppose Susan didn't have a compelling reason, but you decide to let her sit it out anyway and replace her with Sarah for this particular project. Everything's going well, but one day you overhear Susan at the watercooler saying Sarah is a terrible human being for working with this client. What do you do now?

In my early years, if I'd faced this situation, I would have deployed accountability and fired Susan, or I would've been delusionally optimistic that it would blow over. In this situation, she declined to work on a project even though she didn't have a compelling reason, I still let her sit out, and yet she's soiling the company's culture and trying to cancel Sarah. That's just not acceptable. If I were faced with this situation now, I would use kind candor first in a one-on-one conversation:

> *Hey, Susan, good to see you. Listen, I've got to be honest. I don't think you gave me a very compelling reason why this client project goes against your personal beliefs. I appreciate that you don't like the brand, but I think it's a project you could've still supported in some capacity. However, even after I accommodated your request and replaced you with Sarah, I've noticed you're damaging our culture. You're poisoning the well by going out of your way to tell the team that Sarah's not a humanitarian, and you're making her feel uncomfortable. We have a real problem here, and I want to explore what we can do about it.*

Now, instead of firing her outright or not addressing it at all, I'd first make it clear to Susan that I notice her negative behavior. I'd give her an opportunity to fix it. If she still continues, then I'd probably let her go.

I would understand where she's coming from, because she's adamantly against this client. Unfortunately for both of us in this scenario, I was not, and it put us in a precarious spot. However, at this point I would have to suffocate the options. If she has decided she doesn't want to be at the company anymore, she must leave, or if she stays, she at least has to not soil the culture based on the decision we made.

»»»

Scenario 28 Follow-Up Question:
"What if Susan did come to your initial conversation with a compelling reason why she didn't want to work on the client project?"

»»»

Then we're good.

In any interaction, I try to first understand the other person's intent. If I believe Susan's being genuinely thoughtful and well-intentioned, then we're good. Forever. That's why I react so viscerally when I feel that people are acting with bad intentions.

At the same time, I know I don't have all the context. That's why accountability and kind candor are crucial for both the CEO and the employee. As a CEO, it's my responsibility to create an environment where Susan feels safe enough to share her honest feelings, thoughts, or insecurities with me. But Susan needs to also be accountable as an employee and communicate with kind candor if she feels that the company isn't doing right by her.

Your job is just one part of your life. If you're not giving kind candor there, are you avoiding it in other areas too? Could your marriage improve with more of it? What about your relationship with your kids, your neighbors, your friends, or even yourself?

Finally, I would say this: there have been multiple times in real life when I have decided against working with a client, and there have been multiple times when an employee's feedback was the driving force for us to walk away.

Scenario 29: You're twenty-three and just finished four years of art school. COVID lockdowns are in place, businesses are struggling, and you don't have a job. You start driving for Uber and Lyft while you're looking for an opportunity. One day, after not getting many rides, you go on Twitter and start noticing people talk about these things called NFTs. After about five hours of reading on social media over two days, you realize, "Holy shit, I can do this!" What would you do next?

———————

One of my favorite things about innovation is that it sometimes gives new opportunities to people who haven't had them in the past.

For example, social media created significant opportunities for influencers. Please go read the *New York Times* bestseller *Crush It! Why NOW Is the Time to Cash In on Your Passion*. I spoke about it twelve years ago. People are now able to make $120,000 a year being an expert on stretching, or $90,000 a year being a chef on the Internet.

People didn't anticipate the long tail, or the money you could make with your expertise. Cash in on your passion. It couldn't have been more accurate.

In this scenario, I'm going to basically write *Crush It!* all over again. NFTs are going to do for artists what social media did for people with personalities.

Artists would normally think about finding jobs in the advertising industry, Hollywood, or some other "creative" field. The truth is, they need to compromise their creativity when they take up those jobs. They're not creating what they want to create at work, not even at VaynerMedia.

This person needs to reassert the ambition of youth. He or she needs to go back to the mind-set of the thirteen-year-old who said, "I'm going to be Banksy one day," the one who at eighteen dreamed of being Michelangelo. Tap into that ambition.

My advice for that artist? This is your moment. This is the time to be tenacious, both in your output and in your networking. Don't underestimate the power of humility. When personalities tried to become influencers on social media, they dreamed of making millions, but many didn't have the humility to land at $88,000 a year and enjoy the shit out of the fact that they get to be social-media influencers.

The same thing will happen to artists. Would you rather be an executive making $110,000 and hating your Monday through Friday, or would you rather make $59,000 per year being a working artist? Do you have the tenacity to fight for your art when you're about to turn thirty in a few weeks and you're still living with a roommate? Or would you compromise and get a job you hate making logos at a brand?

I know millions and millions of artists are going to be benefited by NFTs. It's the option economy: they have new ways to monetize their passion now.

The number of people pre-NFT who could earn $219,000 a year as artists is a fraction of those who will be able to in 2031. Creatives at ad firms or on Broadway who now earn $110,000 a year to make things they're not passionate about could potentially replicate that same income making what they dream of making. Or they could earn $59,000 and still be so much happier.

Technology is about to create an opportunity that we haven't seen in the history of mankind. I'm so happy and excited for all you artists who are reading.

Tenacity is the most important ingredient here. I don't want anyone to give up along the way. When an artist launches his or her first NFT project and it sells zero pieces when it cost money to mint them, that person will curse me out in an e-mail (gary@vaynermedia .com) and say, "Fuck you, Gary! You inspired me to do this, but I lost." That's when tenacity should kick in.

Dear artist, here's my message back to you:

DO NOT E-MAIL ME UNTIL YOUR 49TH PROJECT HAS FAILED. Don't even consider it. Otherwise, you've completely missed the point of tenacity. You want to be a working artist and you gave up after one time? Let me get this straight: You want to spend your whole life drawing, painting, coloring, or doodling, and you gave up because nobody paid attention to your very first project? Get out of here.

I want every single artist to have patience and understand that they may have sixty or seventy more years of living if they're starting out at twenty-nine. In that context, what is happiness? Is happiness having your own apartment? Is it having nicer clothes?

Please don't map your actions to fulfill your mom's and dad's ambitions for you to be at a certain place by thirty.

––––––

Scenario 30: You're a forty-seven-year-old who's crushed the last seven years at the office due to some really smart work. You're the head of marketing of an insurance company. You stumbled upon GaryVee five years ago, and your LinkedIn game has improved. You're making $250,000 per year, up from $130,000. You're even starting to get even more vacation time, and your work-life balance is perfect.

But every time you go to sleep at night, you think, *What if I branched off and worked for myself?* You know there are a couple of people at the company who'd be interested in quitting and working with you. The thought of owning 33 percent of your own business along with two partners sounds far more lucrative and exciting. What would you do?

———

The beauty of this scenario is that you have options. Many people don't, so the first move is gratitude.

I wish more people in this situation were optimistic. I'm often confused why people in great situations don't try to achieve something greater when they have the itch. The reality is, if you quit your job, work for yourself, and fail in two years (which often happens), you'll go back into the workforce as a more attractive candidate. You won't just have impressive corporate experience; you'll have entrepreneurial experience too. In several years, that will continue to be valuable. When you start with gratitude, patience, and conviction, you can deploy tenacity to chase your ambitions.

I actually believe this is a no-lose situation. If you're a well-paid senior executive who has the humility to live a lifestyle with low expenses, you can save money to give yourself eighteen to twenty-four months of runway. You can take the leap, scratch your itch, and if you realize you weren't meant to be a founder or CEO, you can get a higher-paying job.

In forty years, the regret of not following your dreams is going to outweigh the pain of quitting your job and failing. Maybe you'll have to live a little more humbly than you already were. Maybe you'll have to take on a small amount of credit card debt after always having money in the bank. Whatever it is, it'll be less painful than being eighty-seven, sitting by yourself, and thinking, *Why did I not start my own company?*

If you felt the chemicals rising in your body when you read this scenario, ask yourself the following question: When you look back at your life in this exact moment, do you regret not asking a certain boy or girl out?

The answer is yes for everybody. Now that you're in your twenties, thirties, forties, or fifties, what was so scary about Sally McGee or Tyrone J saying no?

Let me save you time: nothing. That's exactly how you're going to feel in your old age. You're going to ask yourself, "Why didn't I take the leap?"

Please call a ninety-year-old you know. Call him or her and talk about these scenarios. Regret is the ultimate pain. Use conviction, ambition, and tenacity to push yourself over the edge in your mind to make the jump you want to make. It might take many conversations with yourself to do it. I hope the words on this page help.

———

Scenario 31: You're a small-business owner who took a bank loan to build your business from scratch. That loan took you almost a decade to pay off. However, you're now debt-free, and the business is finally turning enough profit for you to upgrade to a slightly larger apartment for you and your family and to improve your lifestyle. Soon after, a natural disaster comes through your town and destroys your office building. What would you do now?

———

I would give myself some time to mourn. I wouldn't beat myself up for needing some time off or for feeling the loss.

Then, I would deploy gratitude as a weapon against that disappointment. I would feel so grateful that I'm still alive and that my family is OK. I don't control Mother Nature, and there's nothing I could've done about the disaster. It is what it is.

Gratitude limits the amount of time I'd spend dwelling on the situation. Then, I'd start going on the offense with conviction and optimism. "If I could build a successful business from zero once, I can do it again. I can absolutely build this up again, and I will."

From there, I would go into accountability. Accountability in this case is asking yourself, "What can I do right now?" You can use it to put yourself in control.

In this case, maybe I could start a YouTube show documenting the comeback. I could e-mail the links to journalists at every local news outlet. If they pick it up, it could become a national news story that might lead to exposure for a grand reopening, a GoFundMe, or something else. I would hold myself accountable to get myself into a mode of building my life back up.

———

Scenario 32: You're looking to grow to a senior leadership position with more responsibility, but you're not getting chances to work on new projects that will expand your skill set. A few colleagues on your team are getting most of the new opportunities, and you suspect your manager is picking favorites. What would you do?

———

To have a healthy, productive discussion with my manager (with kind candor), I would need to get myself into a positive mental state. I'd use a mix of gratitude and optimism first. In a world where millions of people don't have a job, I actually have one. Even if I'm going through a rough patch, some disagreements with my boss, I would never let myself be confused about my rank out of 7.7 billion people in terms of overall well-being. I have a job in a world where millions of people don't have one at all, and that means I have an opportunity to improve our relationship.

Imagine if your immediate reaction was the opposite:

"Oh, the boss is just picking favorites again."

"He doesn't know how to spot good talent."

"This company's leadership is clueless."

If you walk into a conversation assuming that the other person is quietly undermining you, you're setting yourself up for an unfavorable outcome. Your emotional ingredients will show through in your tone and energy, and the smart ones around you will intuitively sense it. You can't trick the emotionally intelligent.

That doesn't mean you shouldn't stand up for yourself. However, far too many people walk into meetings with employees, bosses, or team members they're having disagreements with and "fight for what's right" without having a single conversation about it first. People approach these convos like an after-school fight.

At VaynerMedia, I've watched employees storm into my office with fire in their eyes, but the second they give me awareness of a difficulty or challenge they're facing, they're stunned how I immediately get on their side. The conversation turns in a positive direction as soon as they bring it to my attention. The fire turns into hearts.

Meanwhile, I wonder how long they've waited to communicate that issue. Have they been sitting on it for seven days? Seven weeks? Seven months? Seven years? How many people left the company without giving themselves or the company the chance to create a fantastic situation?

People allow resentment to fester in their minds while they toss and turn at night, or dump their anger on their parents when they call. It could not be unhealthier.

»»»

Scenario 32 Follow-Up Question:
"What would you say if you were to sit down and talk to the manager? Would you ask for more opportunities?"

»»»

Before asking for anything, I'd gut-check it with humility and self-awareness. There's too much entitlement in the world today.

I've had employees come to my office guns a-blazing, asking for promotions at twenty-two years old, with no experience, having been at the company six months. Some people ask for more responsibility on important projects even though six of the last seven clients they worked with didn't renew. I could still give those people one out every five or six projects, but as a business owner, I'm concerned. Will our growth slow down if I hand them more responsibility when they haven't delivered?

In this scenario, humility and self-awareness are effective filters. What are you actually asking for? Do your results back that up? Or have you become delusional because you have an upcoming wedding, so now you're expecting a business to take care of you? Have you done a little rope-a-dope in your own mind that you deserve a promotion or a raise because of your own life events?

With humility, self-awareness, gratitude, and optimism, you can deliver the following lines to the manager:

> *Hey, manager, I know there are a lot of new initiatives at the company, and there are many talented people in this organization. But I just wanted to bring this to your attention: I noticed you're giving most of the new projects to Bob. I'm not going to be able to show you how great I am unless you give me opportunities too. Is there anything I can do to earn that?*

Scenario 33: You're the owner of your own company, and you're in the process of building a new product offering for your customers. You have a release date for the product in the coming weeks, and you've prepared an e-mail blast to let your customers know. It's very important for the company that this launch goes well. Unfortunately, a junior team member, Sally, accidentally sends that e-mail blast out a week early, before the product is even available. What would you do?

———

Right before Sally walks into my office, I'm probably screaming, *"Fuck!"*

This scenario is a tough one. I like to say that 99 percent of things don't matter. Most of the issues people face in business are blown out of proportion. However, this scenario is really painful. You never get a second chance to make a first impression, and messing up a product launch can be very detrimental to the company.

As the owner of the company, I would truly be disappointed. I would immediately scream "Fuck!" because I would need to release my disappointment *before* talking to Sally.

After you get such news, maybe your style is to take a long run or have a hard workout. Maybe you punch a punching bag. You need to get your frustration out, so you don't blow up on your employee.

Then, I would assess the situation through the lens of accountability. I hired the person who hired the person who hired the person who hired Sally. I created the framework that allowed her to make that mistake. How can I fall into a spiral of blaming others when I'm the source?

My top priority at that moment wouldn't be to give the team

critical feedback. It would be to make Sally feel safe. She's probably terrified and spinning out of control, thinking, *I'm about to get fired.*

The best way to react is with a huge dose of empathy. As soon as she walks into my office or as soon as I make that FaceTime call, I'd quickly put her at ease by saying, "Everything is going to be OK."

That conversation is my opportunity to create safety. If you want to deliver feedback to the junior team member with kind candor, you can do it later, when things have cooled down. Giving feedback when you're emotionally on tilt could have a more pernicious influence on the team.

Shouting "You all ruined this for me" is just going to instill more fear, which means the team will feel inhibited. People will be looking over their shoulders, casting blame instead of taking accountability, holding back new ideas out of fear. The company will grow more slowly, which would be a far bigger problem than one failed product launch. When people feel safe, they go on the offense. Going on the offense leads to growth.

Once safety has been created, the question then becomes, "How can we spin this into a positive?"

This is where gratitude comes in. Now that I've gotten my frustrations out and had conversations with my team, I'd have an improved perspective on the mistake and recognize that it's not that serious. Maybe I could make a fun video bantering with my junior employee and send it out to my e-mail list:

Me: *"This is Sally. She hit Send by accident. Jeeeez! We're really sorry; we don't have the product yet. We'll be back next week with*

the official announcement and a special discount code for you:
SallyMessedUp. Look for it! Right, Sally?"
Sally: *"Ha ha. Right, boss!"*

There's always an opportunity to make lemonade from lemons.

Scenario 34: Over a three-year period, you and your husband turn a side hustle selling virtual art classes into a full-time company. You both have been putting out content on Instagram, TikTok, and LinkedIn. The business has rapidly grown to $300,000 in yearly revenue. You and your husband have complementary skills and a successful fifty-fifty partnership. However, your husband is now happy with where the company is at, while you have ambitions to grow it to seven figures and beyond. What would you do?

I watch so many people struggle in marriages, business partnerships, and relationships because they're frustrated with their partner's level of ambition.

In this scenario, your husband has new data. He now feels that he wants to enjoy a little bit of his money. He might say, "You know what, I'm happy making $180k profit on this $300k revenue. Instead of reinvesting it to get us to a million, I want to do things like go to Disney World with the kids and stay at a nice hotel."

As his wife and business partner, you might find those words difficult to hear, especially if you had conversations in the early days about how the two of you both would take this business to $10 million in revenue someday.

When you're in a partnership, though, empathy and humility come first, not conviction. When you sit down to have a talk with your husband about your different ambitions, you can't be in an aggressive, ego-driven mental state. Notice how ingredients like conviction, tenacity, and ambition are almost never the first go-to reactions in difficult scenarios. That's because you can't counter aggression with aggression right away; you need to defuse it first.

Starting with empathy and humility sets you up to have a productive conversation. When you're empathetic and humble, it's hard to aim negative energy at other people. In this scenario, that means recalling everything your husband has done for the business to help you get to $300,000 per year. Even though you have differing opinions now, you wouldn't have gotten to this point without him.

It's OK that your husband is content with the current revenue. It's also OK that you want to take it to a million. You don't need to compromise on your goals and happiness. You also don't need to convince your husband to change his. Together you can create a two-part structure to make this work:

1. Hire someone to do your husband's job.

2. Look at the bigger picture of everything your husband is helping you with.

The first part is easy. You sit down with your husband, break down everything he's doing to help the business, and hire someone, so he can take a break.

At first, you'll feel relieved because you found a solution. Seven months later, when you're burning the midnight oil preparing for an art class after putting the kids to bed and your husband is sitting there playing Call of Duty with his time off, you'll feel like wringing his neck.

That's when you need to take a step back. Look at how he's helping you in life, not just in the context of business. Is he taking care of the household? Is he picking the kids up from soccer practice while you do your virtual sessions? Is he helping them with homework while you're running the company?

Even if he's not directly involved in the company, he could be setting you up to win at life in a different way.

———

Scenario 35: **You're fifteen, and you're making about $1,400 a week from trading sports cards. You're a straight-A student at school, but your grades are now starting to slip. You're also less interested in lacrosse, even though you're a freshman on the varsity team positioned for Ivy League schools. Your new sports-card addiction is keeping you up late at night, and you'd rather spend time trading than studying, playing lacrosse, or enjoying casual escapism like Fortnite. What do you do?**

———

This scenario is a fun one for me. I have so many kids hitting me up about similar situations in their own lives, scared they're screwing up their futures. Somewhere around seventh to ninth grade, a framework was established: *I'm an exceptional lacrosse player, and that's my life path,* or *I'm an exceptional student, and that's how I'm going to win.*

Usually, this is the result of a family dynamic that can be healthy in some ways but unhealthy in others. Some parents look at their fifteen-year-old kid like a product. They say, "This is my Harvard daughter," or "This is my lacrosse-player son."

Depending on what the parents do for a living, they may have different subconscious ambitions for their children. If the parents are entrepreneurs, they may be comfortable with their kid trading sports cards. If they're academics or executives, it may make them uncomfortable.

Here's what I would tell the kid in this scenario:

Have empathy for yourself. It's OK to have these feelings. Maybe you're actually an entrepreneur, or maybe you have entrepreneurial tendencies. Either way, have empathy for your parents. They have an ideology for you, and you're fucking it up. You need to be empathetic so you can absorb their criticism and any attempts to manipulate the situation.

For example, they might tell you, "We'll pay you $1,400 a week. Don't even worry about the cards." You need to be accountable and self-aware and realize that will lead you to a spoiled life. Don't let that happen.

The reps you're getting in the trenches are worth more than the money. Focus on patience and conviction. You need to be OK with getting B's instead of A's for the time being.

At the same time, you may go through this sports-card phase for twelve months and grow out of it by sophomore year. You may have to work harder to improve the grades that you let slip at fifteen. You'd need conviction that you can get back to a decent GPA if you double down in second semester sophomore year, if and when you stop caring about sports cards. Take the steam out of the anxiety that comes with choosing between two options. You're not choosing between grades or sports cards; you're choosing in the short term. You can catch back up.

One example of this is my physical well-being. I was behind everybody in my twenties and thirties, but strong execution with a personal trainer for seven years allowed me to catch up, although probably not all the way, compared to where I'd be if I'd been training hard from my early twenties. But my point is, people are fearful of choosing, but in reality, the decision isn't final. It's not either-or. You can do both.

When your peers make fun of you for getting worse at lacrosse and letting your grades fall, use a combination of humility, conviction, self-awareness, and accountability to deal with it. You're the one who wanted to trade sports cards. You're the one who followed your beliefs and made the decision to let other areas of your life slide for the time being. Even if your sports-card phase throttles your ability to play lacrosse at a top college while your friends are getting recruited, recognize that it wasn't a waste of time. Nor was it the worst thing that ever happened to you.

Even if your goals change in junior year compared to where you are at fifteen, you'll eventually become more aware of how valuable the lessons were from your sports-card years. As a junior or senior, you might be pissed at yourself for screwing up your freshman year on paper, but at twenty-five when you join a startup, those skills you learned from fifteen to sixteen are going to come to the fore. Patience.

Look at your life in a hundred-year window, not a hundred-day window.

———

Now it's your turn. Post a video on the social-media platform of your choice describing a challenging real-life scenario you faced in your career, how you handled it then, and how you would handle that situation differently today. Use the hashtag #ScenariosGaryVee when you post it.

PART III

Exercises

Before you can properly combine these ingredients in your own life situations, you need to develop each one individually. Here you'll find a handful of exercises you can use as a starting point to build your emotional capacity and improve on your halves. You'll find exercises to help you with every ingredient listed in part I, including kind candor.

Some of these exercises will be easy for you. Others might be more challenging.

GRATITUDE

Turn on your phone's selfie camera and record a video saying something like this:

I'm making this video to tell you the five things that are most important to me in the world. These are things that I'm so thankful and grateful for. I want you to send this video back to me anytime I complain about something minor.

Text that video to the five to fifteen people you talk to the most.

I want to compel you to care about the health and well-being of your family over everything. When gratitude is grounded in that, you'll see how easy it is to navigate through challenges in your career.

SELF-AWARENESS

For this exercise, I want you to answer a few questions about yourself and how you'd typically respond in a variety of different situations in both business and life. Then, send those questions to the ten people closest to you professionally and personally through an anonymous Google Form that they can fill out.

This way, you'll get a sense for your level of self-awareness and how your perception of yourself compares to how others see you. Head over to garyvee.com/selfawareness for the full instructions (including the questions and how to set up the Google Form).

ACCOUNTABILITY

Think about a time recently when you deflected blame on someone else for something that was your fault.

Post a video or photo on the social-media platform where you have the most followers and apologize for it. Use the hashtag #AccountabilityGaryVee. I'll be scrolling through and giving love to as many of you as I can!

OPTIMISM

Open your phone contacts and find the five people in your address book whom you deem the most optimistic.

Text them and ask to set up a fifteen-minute conversation. Ask them why they're so optimistic. Ask them to use specific examples.

I believe that the more you hear other humans talk about optimism, the more you can formulate your own context and understanding of it. I've honed many skills in my life by surrounding myself with people who are strong in those areas.

P.S. This exercise could also lead to a conversation with somebody you haven't talked to in a while. That's always nice too.

EMPATHY

Call one close family member and one close friend from work.

Ask them, "From our interactions in the last few years, can you give me an example of a time when you were upset about something, and my reaction didn't bring you value? Was there a time when my reaction to an event poured lighter fluid on your stress or anxiety? Tell me the story."

You'll hear about a time when another human being was hurt because you were unable to empathize, being more focused on yourself than the other person.

KINDNESS

Practice allocating part of your time and part of your finances for kindness:

1. Go on GoFundMe.com and donate what you can afford to a cause that touches your heart.

2. Donate your time and your skills. This is one I'll challenge myself on too. If you're fortunate enough to have achieved great financial success, it's easy to donate $1,000, $10,000, or even $100,000 to a charity. That's why I've always felt that the kindest acts I do are the random one-hour meetings I give to people. Even though I still make those financial donations, the greatest value I can give is my time.

Kindness is based on the recipient's terms. Not yours.

KIND CANDOR

Kind candor was actually the most difficult ingredient for me in this book. It's still a half, not even a full ingredient.

For this exercise, think about someone in your life you need to talk to with kind candor. Then write out an e-mail as though you were talking to him or her in person, and send it to kindcandor @veefriends.com.

TENACITY

Go on YouTube right now and type in "good form push-ups" and watch a video to get educated. Then do as many push-ups as you can in a row, and post a video on your social-media platform of choice with how many you did.

I want you to do push-ups every day for fifty-five days. On the fifty-fifth day, make another video talking about how many push-ups you can do then, and use the hashtag #GaryVee55Days at that point, so I can find it!

I believe that the mind and body are deeply intertwined, and that physical exercise can have profound effects on your mental state.

CURIOSITY

On your social-media platform of choice, post a video telling your followers that you're on a curiosity mission. Ask them to send you a link to a Wikipedia article or a YouTube video of something they're passionate about but don't think you know about. Use the hashtag #CuriosityGaryVee.

Allocate twenty hours to reading, listening, or watching videos on topics you've never considered before at the recommendation of those who are somewhat close to you. Make a commitment to curiosity, even if that means what you're learning about isn't the most interesting. One subtle input may trigger something that benefits you in an unexpected way.

PATIENCE

1. Using a calendar tool (Google Calendar or some other app), create an event titled "You still have plenty of time." Set it so that it pops up on your calendar every six months at 9:00 a.m. for the next ten years.

2. Post positive statements about your ten-, twenty-, or thirty-year goals on your favorite social-media channel. Communicate how excited you are to still be on your journey decades from now. Use the hashtag #PatienceGaryVee.

I make a lot of comments about how I'm going to be an OG in my seventies or how I'm just getting started at forty-six. These stories I tell myself create a beautiful narrative around patience. I don't picture myself being eighty and sick in a retirement home. I picture myself at eighty giving a keynote, looking at all the fresh faces in the crowd, and feeling just as curious about what they're thinking as I'd feel now.

CONVICTION

Write down one strong belief that you've doubled down on over time:

_____

_____

Write down a belief you had that you've wavered from:

_____

_____

From this exercise, what did you learn about conviction? Make a quick video with your thoughts, post on your social-media platform of choice, and hashtag it #ConvictionGaryVee.

HUMILITY

Spend five minutes writing down every single thing you're not good at. Then cut out the page and hang it on your fridge, frame it in your bedroom, or put it next to your mirror. I want you to look at it every day. When you're done writing, take a picture of this page and share it on social media with #HumilityGaryVee.

_____

_____

_____

_____

_____

_____

_____

_____

_____

_____

_____

_____

_____

_____

AMBITION

I want to challenge you to record a selfie video talking about your biggest ambition in life. Post it on social media using the hashtag #AmbitionGaryVee.

In this exercise, I'm trying to make you accountable to your ambition. By putting yourself in a vulnerable position where others can make fun of you if you don't achieve your ambition, you can work on not being mentally vulnerable to that judgment.

CONCLUSION

When you develop these twelve and a half ingredients to your maximum potential, working from nine to five might even be too many hours in the day. Seriously.

As you develop kind candor, gratitude, self-awareness, accountability, optimism, empathy, kindness, tenacity, curiosity, patience, conviction, humility, and ambition, you begin to work with minimal friction. Your colleagues feel safe, happy, and calm around you, speeding up execution.

When these ingredients are instilled properly throughout an organization, team members won't have to spend thirty minutes in a seven-minute meeting. They won't feel the need to invite eight extra people because of insecurities and politics. Those who need to be in a meeting can be there, others can focus on their tasks, and projects can move faster.

By taking accountability for your actions, you can skip the two-week dark spiral of blaming others for a bad business decision. With self-awareness, you can focus on your strengths instead of spending your whole life checking the boxes on your weaknesses. By practicing gratitude, you can limit the time spent dwelling on mistakes. With empathy, kindness, and humility, you won't be fazed when insecure people try to drag you down. When you're optimistic, curious, and patient, you can lead with trust and create scale. With kind candor, you can communicate feedback before resentment develops. All those ingredients will help you operate with tenacity and conviction as you move toward your ambitions.

The funny thing is, even though your job won't take forty hours a week, you might find yourself still working at eight p.m. because you're having so much fun. Strong emotional structure leads to speed in business and life. By mixing these ingredients appropriately, you can move without your fears limiting every step.

When Raghav read off the ingredients to get my initial take on each for part I, my immediate reaction was always "*This* is the one. *This* ingredient is the foundation for success."

That reminded me that every one of the attributes I laid out is essential, and they are all interdependent. None of them can operate in silos. The scenarios in part II were my best attempt at thinking through how they would be deployed in the realities we all go through. It's the mixture that will lead to success. You're the chef.

I've always emphasized tenacity in my content, because it's the most controllable variable for most people. It's often more challenging to become empathetic, humble, or self-aware. Developing these ingredients takes a lot of practice if they don't come naturally to you. The exercises in part III are just a starting point. You might have to analyze your childhood, maybe even go to therapy. I've been aware of my lack of candor for over twenty years, but I'm just now developing it in my mid-forties. This stuff takes time.

For most people, it's easier and faster to put in a few extra hours to achieve their ambitions. However, tenacity out of balance is counterproductive, because it can bring fatigue, burnout, or lack of sleep. It needs to be used in combination with self-awareness and conviction.

As you begin to use these attributes in the workplace, you'll start using them outside the workplace too. All of a sudden, you'll notice that you didn't buy something you didn't need, because you're patient. If the neighbor's dog runs over to your yard and takes a shit, you'll make a joke with kind candor and bond over it, instead of fighting.

Imagine the typical reaction to that classic Americana story. Unhappy people will compound their own unhappiness by shouting at the neighbor for not keeping the dog on a leash. The relationship gets smeared, and it becomes awkward every time they see each other in the backyard. All for what? Because the neighbor came home after a long day at work and forgot to put the dog on a leash?

This entire book could've just been one line: "Are you insecure?" This was my effort to put a mirror in front of you and ask you that question in dozens of different ways through real-life scenarios and exercises.

You can see why I always deploy the most empathy and kindness to the nastiest people. They're adding to their own unhappiness with their bad behavior. Those are broken, insecure individuals who often project their own unhappiness onto somebody else who's also unhappy, and they both start arguing. That's what happens at many companies, and that's what I'm trying to change with this book.

I've noticed that people sometimes demonize business. Occasionally, society sees businesspeople as the opposite of these twelve and a half ingredients. I'm sad that people think business leaders are egotistical, take advantage of others, and use their success as an excuse to be mean to everyone around them. It's actually why most customers are afraid to trust businesses. If I can use my popularity and this moment in time to change how business is branded, I can change a lot of things.

Some reading this sentence right now are ready to quit their jobs, and it'll be the best thing they ever did. Others are currently uncovering their insecurities and will come into the office tomorrow slightly humbler. Still others are about to get promoted for the next seven straight years because they've realized they've been complainers, but now they'll start being more accountable.

But best of all, their lives will feel lighter.

There are different forms of privilege in society, but the ultimate privilege is peace of mind. I hope this book will help you get there.

THE INSPIRATION BEHIND THIS BOOK

The time lag in releasing this book after *Crushing It!* was large in my author career because I felt at the time that my next book had the potential to be thoughtful. It had the potential to be deeper than anything I'd ever written. I could just sense it.

I had a lot of different topics I was debating. If you follow my social-media content closely, you know how excited I am about writing a parenting book from the perspective of a child who's incredibly happy with his parents. I continue to give a lot of thought to a book to be called *Jab Jab Jab Left Hook*, a sequel to *Jab Jab Jab Right Hook*. The concept of making contextual creative for platforms continues to be an incredibly important conversation as platforms like TikTok and Clubhouse emerge and platforms like LinkedIn and Snapchat evolve.

However, when I was at USC, I met Mikey Ahdoot, a young man with a lot of passion and gusto whom I intuitively felt good about. I've met many high-energy people who pitch me many things, and I don't always feel great about it. They're mostly coming from a place of self-interest, which is OK, but you can't come *only* from a place of self-interest. In this case, I felt it was a bit bigger.

Mikey has a company you should check out called Habit Nest, which produces guided journals that help people build better habits.

Habit Nest's initial pitch to me was that we need a GaryVee journal to break down some of the loftier concepts I talk about in a more tactical way. The idea of creating a journal or a textbook for my audience was intriguing and a good complement to the other content I put out.

Over the years, I've found myself being in two different kinds of projects:

1. Projects that flow fast from idea to production. Going from idea to production sometimes can be very quick even for big projects like my K-Swiss deal, my first book deal, *The #AskGaryVee Show*, or *Overrated/Underrated*.

2. Projects that I have to work through. For example, WineText was in my own head for years before I launched it for my dad.

This book was the second kind. Habit Nest worked on some initial versions with Team GaryVee over the course of a couple of years and made some important contributions. However, as Raghav and I worked on it, it evolved into a very different book—one that tries to map the emotional intelligence that I think is required to win in the next century of business. The concepts in this book will become a massive conversation in culture.

I wanted Mikey and Habit Nest to be recognized for contributing to this project.

ACKNOWLEDGMENTS

First, I want to thank my family, whom I love more than breathing.

Second, I want to thank Raghav Haran: my writer for this book, my collaborator, and my right hand throughout the entire production process. This book could never have been what it is without him.

I want to also thank Mikey Ahdoot, Habit Nest, and everyone on Team GaryVee who contributed.

Finally, thank you to Hollis Heimbouch and the entire Harper-Collins team, who have, once again, been true partners in releasing this book.

NOTES

1. "Gratitude," Lexico, Oxford Dictionaries, https://www.lexico.com/en/definition/gratitude.

2. *WHO Global Water, Sanitation and Hygiene Annual Report 2019* (Geneva: World Health Organization, 2020), https://www.who.int/publications/i/item/9789240013391.

3. Zoë Roller et al., *Closing the Water Access Gap in the United States: A National Action Plan* (Oakland, CA: US Water Alliance; Los Angeles, CA: Dig Deep, 2019), http://uswateralliance.org/sites/uswateralliance.org/files/publications/Closing%20the%20Water%20Access%20Gap%20in%20the%20United%20States_DIGITAL.pdf.

4. Cindy Holleman, ed., *The State of Food Security and Nutrition in the World: Safeguarding against Economic Slowdowns and Downturns* (Rome: Food and Agriculture Organization, 2019), https://www.fao.org/3/ca5162en/ca5162en.pdf.

5. Walk Free Foundation, *Global Slavery Index 2018*, "Highlights" (Perth, Western Australia: Walk Free Foundation, 2018), https://www.globalslaveryindex.org/2018/findings/highlights.

6. "7 Fast Facts about Toilets," UNICEF, Nov. 19, 2018, https://www.unicef.org/stories/7-fast-facts-about-toilets.

7. Joseph Johnson, "Global Digital Population as of January 2021," Statista, Hamburg, Apr. 7, 2021, https://www.statista.com/statistics/617136/digital-population-worldwide.

8. "21 Million Americans Still Lack Broadband Connectivity," Pew Charitable Trusts, Philadelphia, June 2019, https://www.pewtrusts.org/-/media/assets/2019/07/broadbandresearchinitiative_factsheet_v2.pdf.

9. "Global Wage Calculator: Compare Your Salary," CNN Business, 2017, https://money.cnn.com/interactive/news/economy/davos/global-wage-calculator/index.html.

10. Thalif Deen, "Women Spend 40 Billion Hours Collecting Water," Global Policy Forum, New York, Aug. 31, 2012, https://archive

.globalpolicy.org/component/content/article/218/51875-women
-spend-40-billion-hours-collecting-water.html?itemid=id#:
~:text=In%20Sub%2DSaharan%20Africa%2C%2071,40%20
billion%20hours%20per%20year.

11. Aaron O'Neill, "Life Expectancy (from Birth) in the United States,
     from 1860 to 2020," Statista, Hamburg, Feb. 3, 2021, https://www
     .statista.com/statistics/1040079/life-expectancy-united-states-all
     -time/#:~:text=Life%20expectancy%20in%20the%20United%20
     States%2C%201860%2D2020&text=Over%20the%20past%20
     160%20years,to%2078.9%20years%20in%202020.

12. "Complacency." Lexico, Oxford Dictionaries, https://www.lexico
     .com/en/definition/complacency.

13. "Self-Awareness," Lexico, Oxford Dictionaries, https://www.lexico
     .com/en/definition/self-awareness.

14. "Accountability," Lexico, Oxford Dictionaries, https://www.lexico
     .com/en/definition/accountability.

15. "Optimism," Lexico, Oxford Dictionaries, https://www.lexico.com
     /en/definition/optimism.

16. "Delusion," Lexico, Oxford Dictionaries, https://www.lexico.com
     /en/definition/delusion.

17. "Pessimism," Lexico, Oxford Dictionaries, https://www.lexico.com
     /en/definition/pessimism.

18. "Empathy," Lexico, Oxford Dictionaries, https://www.lexico.com
     /en/definition/empathy.

19. "Kindness," Lexico, Oxford Dictionaries, https://www.lexico.com
     /en/definition/kindness.

20. "Pushover," Lexico, Oxford Dictionaries, https://www.lexico.com
     /en/definition/pushover.

21. "Tenacity," Lexico, Oxford Dictionaries, https://www.lexico.com
     /en/definition/tenacity.

22. "Curiosity," Lexico, Oxford Dictionaries, https://www.lexico.com
     /en/definition/curiosity.

23. "Patience," Lexico, Oxford Dictionaries, https://www.lexico.com
     /en/definition/patience.

24. "Conviction," Lexico, Oxford Dictionaries, https://www.lexico.com
     /en/definition/conviction.

25. "Humility," Lexico, Oxford Dictionaries, https://www.lexico.com
     /en/definition/self-awareness.

26. "Ambition," Lexico, Oxford Dictionaries, https://www.lexico.com
     /en/definition/ambition.

ABOUT THE AUTHOR

Gary Vaynerchuk is a serial entrepreneur and serves as the chairman of VaynerX, the CEO of VaynerMedia, and is the creator and CEO of VeeFriends. Gary is considered one of the leading global minds on what's next in culture, relevance, and the internet. Known as GaryVee, he is described as one of the most forward thinkers in business—he acutely recognizes trends and patterns early to help others understand how these shifts impact markets and consumer behavior. Whether it is emerging artists, esports, NFT investing, or digital communications, Gary understands how to bring brand relevance to the forefront. He is a prolific angel investor with early investments in companies such as Facebook, Twitter, Tumblr, Venmo, Snapchat, Coinbase, and Uber.

Gary is an entrepreneur at heart—he builds businesses. Today, he helps Fortune 1000 brands leverage consumer attention through his full-service advertising agency, VaynerMedia, which has offices in New York, Los Angeles, London, Latin America, and Singapore. VaynerMedia is part of the VaynerX holding company, which also includes VaynerProductions, VaynerNFT, Gallery Media Group,

The Sasha Group, VaynerSpeakers, VaynerTalent, and Vayner-Commerce. Gary is also the cofounder of VaynerSports, Resy, and Empathy Wines. He guided both Resy and Empathy to successful exits—they were sold to American Express and Constellation Brands, respectively. He's also a board member at Candy Digital and a cofounder of VCR Group.

In addition to running multiple businesses, Gary documents his life daily as a CEO through his social media channels, which have more than thirty million followers across all platforms. His podcast *The GaryVee Audio Experience* ranks among the top podcasts globally. He is a five-time *New York Times* bestselling author and one of the most highly sought-after public speakers. He serves on the board of MikMak, Bojangles Restaurants, and Pencils of Promise. He is also a longtime Well Member of charity: water.